Who the Fuck Am I

Ancestry Answers

Tara J Powell

DEDICATION

This book is dedicated to my family.

Past, Present and Future

Thank You
for everything you have been and done for me and for everything
you will be and do because of me

Table of Contents

Part 1.   WTF is Wrong with Me?
Chapter 1   My Family Makes Me Miserable
Chapter 2   No one Loves Me or Even Likes Me A Little Bit
Chapter 3   I'm Not Good Enough & I Don't Fit in Anywhere
Chapter 4   I Have No Idea Who I Am or Why I'm Here

Part 2.   WTF Makes Me Feel This Way?
Chapter 5   21st Century Societies Do Not Benefit from Meaningful Relationships
Chapter 6   Modern Family Meltdown
Chapter 7   Therapy Helps but I'm Still Alone
Chapter 8   Medicine Doesn't Fix Lonely

Part 3.   WTF Can I Do About It?
Chapter 9   Mental Movement Keeps You from Self Hate
Chapter 10   Find the Family that Feels Right
Chapter 11   My Ancestors are Awesome
Chapter 12   How Far We've Come
Chapter 13   How Our Ancestors Lived Together

Part 4.   WTF Should We Do Now?
Chapter 14   We Need Their Strength and Determination Today
Chapter 15   Unite Through Ancestry and Save Our Mental Health

Chapter 16 Bonus Material

1. Links to DNA Testing Companies and Sites
2. Links to Mental Health Data and Statistics
3. Mental Health Help Lines and Connections
4. Coping Mechanisms
5. Connect with Me

Part 1

WTF is Wrong with Me?

I had a fight with my daughter today. It started in the stupidest way but neither of us would back down because we both felt that we were right. I screamed and yelled and said things I didn't mean. I was trying to get my point across but ended up so far from what I was trying to say.

We were planning to go out to dinner for her eighteenth birthday and she wanted to make plans with her friend afterwards. I felt like she didn't appreciate what we were trying to do and the time we wanted to spend with her. It felt like she didn't even want to spend time with us.

By the end of the day she hated me. I had turned a beautiful thing into this disturbing display. If she didn't want to hang out with me earlier she definitely wouldn't want to now.

Why did I do that to her, why did I make her feel that way? We were supposed to be celebrating her big day but instead I made it all about me.

1

My Family Makes Me Miserable

"A family can be the bane of one's existence. A family can also be most of the meaning of one's existence. I don't know whether my family is bane or meaning, but they have surely gone away and left a large hole in my heart." — *Keri Hulme*

My parents weren't good at being parents, they weren't even good at being adults. We had a rough time. Bouncing around being homeless and having to stay with family members plagued my adolescence. It was practically impossible to go to school and fit in. I was usually a little dirty and very socially awkward. I had emotional issues on top of mental instability.

My parents were drinkers and they didn't fit in well either. The drinking only made it harder to get anything accomplished and tore a bigger riff between us. It was also the only thing that got them through the day. I understand this, now, more than I did back then.

I grew up feeling out of place. There was no place for me. I was a burden on everyone around me. There is nothing like having to beg for food, a ride to school or to do your laundry at someone else's house when you're a kid. It really messes with your head.

Who the Fuck Am I?

As I got older, I found ways to get money to tend to some of my own needs but still felt like a burden and an outcast. I've struggled with depression and anxiety most of my life and have always felt like I was running outside of the general social structure. I felt like I could disappear and no one would even notice unless they were thankful they didn't have to deal with me anymore.

In adulthood, I started to think about my past. I realized how much I had blamed my parents, grandparents and siblings for everything. Everything I had gone through alone, the trauma I had experienced and the mental health issues that stemmed from them must have been their faults, right? Did they even know how much I suffered?

I thought my husband and I were doing so much better than our parents had done for us and we were. We were also dealing with our own problems. Our kids were being traumatized by our mental issues just the same. If I'd only known, I probably couldn't have done anything differently and my parents probably couldn't either.

When I started doing my ancestry research it really opened my eyes. The circumstances my parents lived in and the things they went through built their mentality and belief systems. Their upbringing molded their choices, habits, successes and failures. The environment and social systems they grew up in affected them more than the one that we lived in when I was growing up. So Many things have changed and it changed them and how they lived.

Just one generation back society was stricter, families were larger and incomes were lower. My grandparents had eleven children and lived on one income. I'm sure their kids went hungry and bills went unpaid but they made it work. My parents survived with their issues and went on to have a family of their own and try to do better by us.

Another generation back, my grandfather didn't even know his father. He was raised by a teen mother and a stepfather, with 10

Who the Fuck Am I?

half siblings of his own. He wasn't treated bad, per say, but he wasn't one of them and never really knew where he came from.

On the other side, my great grandfather died of appendicitis at the young age of 39 with seven kids. His wife was unable to care for the children and they were taken by the state and put up in a work house in Chicago until they reached 21 years of age. Imagine what that did to their sanity!!

As I looked back further and discovered more of my family history, I found that there were so many cases of families being ripped apart and children being scattered to the wind. Homelessness was less of an outrage back when wars and the great depression ravished the country.

I also learned that, way back when, people used to drink because the water carried so much bacteria that alcohol was a safer bet, even for children. It was also used staggeringly to drown people's sorrows, of which they had many. I started to understand that my parents weren't purposely punishing me or even trying to be bad parents. They were trying to get by and deal with the situations they found themselves in with the skills they had gained in a different world.

Every generation we get more advanced and have new technologies. It's easy for older people to get lost and not be able to find their way through the insanity that is the future. I find myself there now. My kids, on the other hand, have always known the internet. It is nothing for them to do everything online or remotely while it is frustrating and confusing for me to get the hang of it.

I am lost in the social atmosphere of de-categorization that is currently arising. I grew up calling an apple and apple and an orange an orange, dogs were its and boys and girls were born different. That is not the world I find myself in today. That is okay, it is actually a good thing for mental health but it is still confusing, to say the least.

Who the Fuck Am I?

Now, I finally understand that it isn't with vengeance or hatred in our hearts that we let our children down but with confusion and angst that we ourselves are let down. Everything we had to learn to fit into society is suddenly being torn away and it is hard to change after being programmed a certain way.

Everyone is trained a certain way to fit in to the society that they are born into and must survive and hopefully thrive in. That is not necessarily cohesive to the previous or the next generation. In modern times, as things are changing faster and faster, we can expect our social norms and mental health to continuously be altered and tested.

It is the way of the world for things to change. People get stuck in their ways. The next generation grows up thinking it is torture only to fall into the same ebb and flow of aging and altered perceptions. We just need to understand it all and that is why I love my ancestry and building my family tree. It exposes my history in a way that is accurate and connective, yet removed, understandable and unbelievable all at the same time!

While our families often fail to meet the mark they really are doing their best to prepare us to be adults. Biologically speaking, humans pass on our genetics and do our best to guarantee the survival of our lines and the advancement of our genetic code in future populations. It's survival of the fittest and everyone subconsciously wants their DNA to make the cut.

In a much more literal sense, most parents want to do the best by their kids. They want to do better than their parents did. Success requires you to fit into society with proper morals and behaviors that connect you to the community in which you live. The major problem with that is that society is ever changing. Preparations are often outdated and seem to be antiquated and useless to the children by the time they learn them.

Parents often push their kids too hard to compete in school or sports. Don't get me wrong, education and physical fitness are both important to healthy development. If the pressure to perform

Who the Fuck Am I?

causes stress or mental anguish though, we must ask ourselves if the outcome is worth the damage caused. If a child feels inadequate and like they are not accepted for their capabilities it can cause complex mental trauma that lasts a lifetime. This trauma will go on to affect generations to come, their upbringing and mental status as well.

This may lead to children acting out or misbehaving at home or in social setting to get the attention they are lacking. We all want to be treated affectionately. It actually causes our brains to release endorphins and pleasure hormones that make us happy. When those behaviors and hormones are not applied, children's minds seek to get some form of interaction or satisfaction. Negative behaviors and negative emotions fill the void and eventually become the normal mental status.

Parents are then faced with the battle of raising good kids verse fighting bad ones. Yelling, screaming, hitting and fighting are all historically common practices to punish children. In the olden days' kids were seen and not heard and if they were heard they could get hit with a belt or switch, sent to bed without dinner or worse. Over the generations, we have learned that many of those treatments caused much worse long lasting behaviors and mental illness than the improper behaviors they were originally a solution to.

Parents are forced to make tough decisions regarding what is acceptable for their kids. This includes behaviors they should learn and be exposed to and what is not ok and will not benefit them in the future. This causes extreme complication during the teenage years, and always has. As children mature, their brains develop towards adulthood and they yearn for interaction and control of their own social bonds. They are not yet mature enough to understand. The wild and fun people and activities are setting them up for failure in the future and that takes us back to the survival of the fittest. Parents will fight, their own children, tooth and nail to keep them away from bad influences and ensure their safety and survival in the years to come.

Who the Fuck Am I?

I always thought that the "stuff" going on in the 90's, when I was a teenager, was the most important thing in the world. Through my ancestry research I learned that every generation has these same battles just over different social situations & expectations. That is what I believe makes life so difficult, in a generational sense.

How does someone that grew up in the 50's, with the Model American Family, know how to raise a child in the 80's or 90's with Cyndi Lauper and Madonna? Then, how too, can that person that grew up in the 80's with social activism and a single-family household know how to raise a child in the new millennium with the internet and both parents working to make a life for them?

It goes back further and further. Life was simpler and families were closer physically but further apart in many ways. Societies grew and advanced. The requirements for survival and success changed. The older generations have been raised in one world, learned success in another and go on to raise children in the next. Sadly, this knowledge can only truly be known from hindsight.

Societies have grown and got busier and busier, especially with both parents working, the basic upbringing of the children has been shrunk down or eliminated altogether. Parents simply don't have time to sit with them, teach them, or train them in the same 24/7 manner that our grandparents did.

These life lessons are becoming the responsibility of babysitters or school districts. Neither of which have the parent's mindset or belief system at the heart of it. They simply want kids to be sufficient in society not necessarily good, moral people that will grow up and survive. They have no steak in the game of genetic dependency.

Parents are no longer the driving force in raising and teaching children. Children then lack the emotional cues and responses to their behaviors that are required for healthy mental development. This often leaves children with an emotional barrier where they simply do not understand when and how to express their feelings.

Who the Fuck Am I?

They bottle up any and all feelings leaving them incapable of creating and interacting within social and personal relationships.

In the small amount of time parents have with their children they choose to ignore poor behaviors and try to focus on the positive. They don't want to be punishing their kids the entire time they spend with them but without structural attention the child feels neglected or abandon. They believe the parent just doesn't care what they do.

This can lead to the "If you can't beat them, join them" mentality where kids decide that they don't have to care or listen to their parents because they don't care or listen to them. Which is a complete backfire because the parent is often trying to enjoy the time they share and build only a positive relationship and it ends up destroying any bond they share.

Historically, families had trauma but they were close. They were all on the same farm, in the same house, in many cases they all shared the same bedroom, parents and children included. There was no escape or ignoring one and other. Life was much more demanding and any falter from social norms could place someone on the chopping block or at the least leave them single and living a rough life of despair, trying to do everything on their own. Without the conveniences of the modern world, life actually demanded that people work together to survive and in many cases, that didn't even work. Life was fragile and survival was not guaranteed.

The stories of my ancestors have made me think about what we are gaining and losing and I know I cannot change it. No one can stop change or make the world stop turning. I have watched the world change over the last 40 years. I cannot recognize the time when I grew up. It is lost and gone forever but the lessons I learned there are real and will impact how I raise my kids and treat my grandchildren for the rest of my days.

This is where we get into, what I call, The Fight. I want to teach my kids how to be good people. I believe they need to get face to face contact with other humans and build strong relationships. I expect them to get married and have children, hence the grandchildren comment in the previous paragraph.

They don't see the importance of any of it. They will be who they want to be and treat people how they want to treat them even if that is not how they want to be treated. They do not see the value in meeting people in person, they do not want to get married and have kids, at least not yet.

My position at the head of the household grants me complete control although I do not actually have it. I must beg and bribe and work in manners that are completely beneath me in an attempt to get them to see things my way. Which they cannot, they did not grow up the way I did or experience the world that I did. How can I expect them to understand the past and pretend that they live then and there, when I actually live in the present and cannot get used to it or understand much of what is normal now?

Hence, we fight. We fight over school, work, dating, the future and even the past. We especially fight over the way of this new world, the cancel culture, the de-categorization, expectations and acceptable behaviors.

Do I want to fight with my children, my meaning for existence, the only ones that can carry my genetic code into the future? Absolutely not, but I do because I am stubborn and stuck in my ways and my brain says that I am right.

This leads me back in time, remembering how many times I fought with my parents over the simplest societal changes I believed then that it would be the end of the world if they didn't let me do…. whatever I wanted that day. Hating them for being so old and dumb and not understanding me and the world I was living in.

Many times, we fell into ignoring each other because if you can't beat 'em join 'em. They just didn't have the fight left in them and I was young and spry, I could fight for hours. Many fights ended in violence and hatred. Not speaking to each other for days and then criticizing and demeaning each other more when we did

Who the Fuck Am I?

speak.

It was absolutely traumatizing for us all. I look back with sadness and guilt for the way I treated them. I also understand that they were the ones responsible for teaching me how to interact and react. Then I feel shame for the damaged family that I come from.

I look at my children and want so badly to go back to a time when we didn't have to fight, when none of us wanted to fight. Perhaps if we'd lived in the 18th century or the 17th or 16th. Maybe back in the 8th century when Vikings were pillaging and raiding. All the way back in the 1st when the bible was being written.

We could have all seen the world in the same light and understood each other and got along. Probably not though, every generation has their problems and differences.

I look at the world that existed in any of those time periods and find that I had ancestors suffering the world they lived in and fighting with their kids over it. Familial trauma has a very cyclic nature. It will always be there, changing with society and our morals and beliefs. The elderly cannot see the world the way the children do and because of their experiences and mindset they will believe that they are right. When defeat draws near, their instincts will kick in and they will fight it out!

It never changes, the human desire to be loved is so strong. When we feel like it is lacking we get angry and turn to hate. Hating ourselves for never being good enough, hating others for not loving us for who we are and most of all hating the world for not being a more loving place. It is extremely counter intuitive if you think about it but I guess all of human nature is.

2

No one Loves Me or Even Likes Me A Little Bit

"We're born alone, we live alone, we die alone. Only through our love and friendship can we create the illusion for the moment that we're not alone." -*Orson Welles*

How do you define love? Is love real or is it just an illusion of the human mind? Is it that gooey stuff they talk about on valentine's day? Is it the controlling nature of someone that says they love you? Is it deep or shallow, platonic or sexual, good or bad?

According to the dictionary, there are several meanings. Love is an intense feeling of affection for someone else. It is also a romantic or sexual attachment It could be a great interest or pleasure in something or someone. You could love a person place or thing. You can use the word love to end a letter or phone call. You can say it to let the other person know that you care.

If you have people that love you, does it make you feel understood or accepted, even wanted? When you love others, and share that love compassionately, do you increase these feelings?

Who the Fuck Am I?

Can being loved and loving others, sharing the love, if I may, decrease the feelings of loneliness, depression, abandonment, etc.? Can Love heal our woes and lead us to a happier and healthier existence?

The need to be loved, seems to be, a purely human attribute. Scientifically speaking, love happens in our brains. A chemical reaction allows hormones to be released causing feelings of bliss, excitement and intense bonding. It doesn't have anything to do with the heart, so why all these pink hearts and broken hearts, heartaches and heart breaks? Humans have really taken this feeling to a whole new level.

There are strong debates on the issue of whether love is instinctual or if it is something that grows over time from a miner connection. We do know, from sociological study, that human populations tend to choose love over hate in a basic sense. We have built this strong bond with our immediate families, friends and even within our communities over millennia.

Love is what has allowed and even encouraged human populations to grow from groups to tribes, clans, villages and eventually to cities, states, provinces and countries. We relate to those within our groups and genuinely care about what happens to them. This compassion has bonded us for our mutual survival.

At the family level, there is love and hate, anger, betrayal, jealousy, joy, happiness, pride, fear and an abundance of other emotions all tangled together within a single household or close familial line. We cannot say every family has strong love for each other or even for every member of the family. Nor can every member hate or be jealous of every other member. This makes me wonder, are families bonded for the survival of the unit or for the self alone?

Do we fend for ourselves and our survival above all else even love? Do pack animals or herding cattle "Love" their families more or do they simply understand that their survival requires large groups to fend off predators. Will they not abandon a lamb that breaks a leg or leave the elderly or stragglers of the herd for the lion so the rest may escape? Does survival require love or create it?

What is survival without love? Is life as gratifying or fulfilling with no one to share it with? Can we go on without compassion or concern? What impacts does a lack of love have on our mental health?

There is research that suggests animals, including humans, feel love for their own offspring so that we care for them and keep them alive. Without that strong feeling of affection and the bond that it brings we would just leave them to die rather than do all the necessary work to keep them alive and bring them to adulthood! If this is true, how do children, that do not get the love that is needed for survival, develop and grow in a world that keeps them alive but not loved?

It seems that love or being loved is the most rewarding feeling we, humans, can get. It, literally, keeps us alive in childhood and nurtures us and allows our minds and emotions to develop properly. Is this true throughout our lives?

Genealogy and ancestry research suggests that a person's importance was measured by the amount of love they gave or received. If they cared for their children well, they were of importance to the family. When they loved the work they did to provide for their families they were important to that families' survival. Loving the everyday tasks and hobbies that kept them busy and taught skills to the next generation made them important to the flow of the family and kept the peace.

We find value in the people that are of importance to our lives. Parents are of value because they kept us alive and taught us to be who we are. Husbands and wives are of value because they give you someone to share your life with, the good and the bad, the duty and joy. Children are valuable because they allow us to pass on the knowledge and skills that we've gained throughout our lives. They also carry our genes on to the next generation and the future of our lineage. We never truly die as long as we pass a part of

Who the Fuck Am I?

ourselves in to the future.

We can take pride in the people and things that we love. Parents are proud of their children when they show the skills we taught them or when they mature to a point beyond our expectations. We can be proud of our job or fitness, sports or other interests. When you are truly dedicated and attached to the feeling that you get from a certain activity, that is love.

Along with pride comes a sense of self-esteem that is personal and rewarding. People often believe that self-esteem is a solely personal emotion and has nothing to do with those around us but that is not true. Often times, our self-esteem is directly based on what others think of us or how they treat us.

If weak self-esteem can stem from bullying or lack of affection, then the opposite is true as well. By showing love and being loved, feeling important to your family and having pride for your contributions you can build positive self-esteem. Building yourself up is the best thing you can do for your own mental health.

This brief description of love and its positive effects on people and families offers understanding of a concept that is often neglected. Does that understanding allow you to share more love in your life? Does lack of that basic understanding allow the neglect of its value in our lives?

Through my research, I have come to find that every generation understands and views our mental health differently. Therefore, they view love differently. Many older people believe that it doesn't matter and life is about the black and white of situations and love falls somewhere on the grey scale in the middle. Others feel that love is only for the lucky, only for men and women, only for children or only for adults. I would argue that love is for every single one of us, in different aspects, of course.

Generation Z is by far the most open about who they want to love but they are lacking the most love and connection with their families. Is this a direct correlation?

Who the Fuck Am I?

They are opening gates that have been blocked by social norms. They push boundaries and want to be free to feel any old kind of way they like. They will free our society from the categories that limit our love and affection. They can help all of their peers find love and feel important and valuable within society. Especially, if they are lacking that connection at home which many of them are. Understanding love, sharing love and being open to love will directly impact the mental health crisis we are experiencing, here in the USA, as well as around the globe in the 21st century.

When we feel a lack of love in our everyday life it negatively effects our mental health which then impacts our quality of life and even our physical health and capabilities. It is easy to fall into the abyss of questioning your own value or worth when you do not have the reassurances of your family, friends or the community to which you are an important part.

3

I'm Not Good Enough & I Don't Fit in Anywhere

"People who cannot invent and reinvent themselves must be content with borrowed postures, secondhand ideas, fitting in instead of standing out." -*Warren Bennis*

What is the gold standard? How do you know if you are good enough or if you will fit in? Humans are genetically and biologically predisposed to judging each other, our environment and in turn ourselves. This characteristic is buried so deep in our genetic code that we may never, truly overcome it. Back in the Hunter Gatherer days, evolution honed this mindset for our very survival.

Humans had to fit in to the pack in order to earn their chance to eat at the communal table, to gather close for warmth and to eventually attract a mate. This was the only way to survive the harsh world they lived in and pass on their genetic code for future generations.

Survival was based on how well a member fit in. Life was dangerous and children learned to immolate the behaviors of their elders in order to make their way through the world with the least amount of risk. They learned to be loud to scare away predators, to be quiet in order to hunt, to be strong when collecting wood for fires or carrying meat back to camp. Imitating others behaviors has always been a defining characteristic to the human mentality.

Do you view yourself as good or bad? Do others view you as good or bad? Does society view you as good or bad? These are the questions that we all ask ourselves to establish if we fit in. We contemplate our options and behaviors in the grand scheme of our life based on these simple questions. The answers will determine our placement in society and have direct impact on our mental health.

If you view yourself as unworthy or like you are not like everyone else within your family or community it affects the way you interact in that group or do not. If you don't fit in with your community, you may resist going out to school or shopping. You may ask others to do things for you and in turn limit your socialization and the ability to "get used to it". Building a sense of sameness with the group is neglected which leaves you with a limited group of individuals to communicate with and a skewed view of your own personality or behavior.

Disassociation from your family makes you feel subjected and different. This differentiation elevates the issues with your mental health pushing you closer to a breaking point. You begin suffering physical symptoms related to your mental status. These symptoms may also occur with public differentiation but is often worse when you feel excluded from your immediate familial group.

The bonding experience that humans have with their families begin at birth. Our parents and grandparents, siblings and aunts and uncles begin to bond with us before our brains have developed the capabilities to form independent bonds. We only have the bond of survival, at birth, and that will attach to anyone that brings us the essential, life sustaining necessities. As we age and grow, we can pick and choose our favorite people or behaviors according to how they make us feel. Mothers often attain the most significant bonds as they are either the primary care giver or because they share more emotional interactions with the children.

Bonds will then shift in and out of any given order based on preference for the rest of our developmental years. These bonds will usually last, the rest of our lives unless there are some extenuating circumstances. The bad part of this is that if these bonds are not formed in youth they often never will be. Leaving the child alone and susceptible to many forms of developmental delays and differences.

When familial bonds are lacking, due to death, neglect, abandonment or busyness the child reaches outside of the familial circle to form dependable bonds with neighbors, friends etc. The human brain knows that we are social beings and depend on others for survival even if that survival is mental rather than physical at this point in our evolutionary existence.

Unfortunately, if a child or young adult is lacking basic social skills or does not assimilate to situations properly, they can be outcast from even the most basic social groupings such as in their own neighborhoods, at school or at work. Without this sense of placement or status our mental health will suffer, leading to despair and withdrawal.

Historically, our families needed each other for more primal and immediate connections so it usually didn't come to this. There would be the rare case of someone that was so far outside of the social norms that they could not possibly be included. Sadly, they would be admitted to insane asylums or completely abandon and nature would be allowed to take its course. In other words, the community or family would let you die if you didn't fit in, by choice or due to some difference or medical or mental condition.

Life was difficult to say the least but the fear of seclusion and death kept our ancestors on their toes. They would fit in at all costs. Even if that meant hiding who they really were. They often would search out opportunities to change themselves to be a better fit for their social situation.

Who the Fuck Am I?

We don't experience this primal life or death exclusion anymore. Learning about it has really opened my eyes to how bad it was for many of my ancestors. Understanding the despair my ancestors suffered allows me to feel a bit of satisfaction even though my life isn't great. The good isn't as good without the bad and we cannot attain greatness without some level of destruction. Our response and reaction to the good and the bad are defined by our experiences with both.

Categorization is both necessary and discriminative at the same time. We understand our surroundings based on a set of categories that we learn in our developmental years. Those categories can be good verse bad, male and female, young and old, active and lazy, smart or dumb, and the list goes on and on and on.

Later in life we get more categories like employed or unemployed, pretty or ugly, happy or sad, healthy or ill, athletic or nerdy. These examples make it seem like all categories are either/or, this or that but in reality, there are many conflicting categories and we either fit in them or not. There are also many categories that are non-inclusive or exclusive meaning that you can be in many categories at ones or none of them at all.

This makes life extremely difficult to navigate and understand yet it is how the human brain works. We must categorize ourselves in order to understand our place in the world and therefor, others place in correlation to our own. We then take all of these judgments and categories and begin stereotyping everyone and everything around us.

People often view stereotypes as an unfair or bias viewpoint of members of a certain group. It can also refer to a type of item or town. Stereotypically, everyone has the same characteristics which define their placement in this category. The cities all have the same crime or poverty or job opportunities or lack thereof. For example, the items are all too big or small or cheap.

Stereotyping allows us to quickly choose between categories and understand a situation or society better. Often it does take an oversimplified point of view. This quick grouping is also known for being too specific in the attributes of a certain category. This leads to discrimination, either purposeful or completely subconsciously.

Discrimination is defined as the loss of one's ability to enjoy their human and/or legal rights equally with others. Basic social discrimination can be based on conformity or lack thereof. If you do not look like the rest of your family or community, you are a nonconformist. You may be discriminated against based on color, gender, weight or height. You may be picked on or bullied, beat up or excluded from social activities based on looks that you can or cannot change.

If you do not act like others in your family or community, you are a non-conformist. You may be discriminated against if you are too obnoxious or too lazy, too loud or too quiet, tell to many jokes or are too serious, if you are too nerdy or too athletic. If you choose to work or to be unemployed, to drink or to do drugs, you can be shunned from society and excluded from common goals and desires within said community.

Historically speaking there was only one real conformity that mattered and that was to the church. If you believed like a good person, a holy person or if you were of the devil. Nonconformists could be banned, excommunicated or even executed based on their religious preferences. The church also used the power of conformity to guide and shape societies to their own liking and benefit.

I am from the United States and in order for my ancestors to immigrate here many of them had to escape religious persecution, based on nonconformity, in other countries. They were Huguenots & Protestants escaping Catholicism, Puritans escaping Protestantism, and once they arrived here the indigenous peoples were persecuted based on their animistic or pagan like spiritual beliefs.

Ethnocentrisms is another form of judgement based on categorization and conformity. Basically, once you find your group you view it as the best group. Others must be lacking since they are not like you. It is a means for humans to qualify and explain ourselves in a positive manner which is extremely healthy from a mental health standpoint but not necessarily true or beneficial to the society as a whole.

For example, every religion believes theirs is the only true and accurate religion, hence they are better than all the others. With over 4000 recognized religions worldwide it is hard for me to tell if any are better or worse than the others and I definitely cannot say which ones are true or accurate!

Another example, the jocks think they are better than the nerds because they are physically fit and can win at whatever sport they play. In turn, the nerds think they are better than the jocks, even if they don't admit or flaunt it, because they are smart and can outthink the jocks in mathematics or sciences.

Self-categorization, stereotyping, conformity and even ethnocentrism create a sense of identification and connection within the social hierarchy. This self-identification produces the characteristics and behaviors that we associate with membership. Yet, todays societies are becoming de-categorized more and more every day and we are losing the simplicity that comes with judgement and classifying the world around us and ourselves.

4

I Have No Idea Who I Am or Why I'm Here

"I can't blame you for trying to categorize me. It's a human instinct. Its why scientists are, to this day, completely flabbergasted by the duck-billed platypus: it's furry like a mammal, but lays eggs like a bird. It defies conventional classification. I AM THE PLATYPUS (Coo coo ka-choo)" — *Jeff Garvin*

Today, a person can be so many things that it is hard to keep up. There are so many decisions and choices that must be made every single day. From an extremely young age through adulthood and extending throughout our lives.

Children are not required to stay in the categories that society has labeled them with. Their parents or themselves can choose almost every single aspect of their reality.

Teens are not expected to fit themselves into the categories their age imposes on them. At such an intriguing and confusing stage of our development, when there have always been a million decisions to be made, teens are now deciding if and who they want to date and how, if or when they want to work and how, many kids are beginning social media careers in these fragile years.

Who the Fuck Am I?

In adulthood, many of these same questions are lagging in people's minds. When our ancestors would have been on their own, married with children our children are still living in our basements. In some cases, raising families with no intention of moving out on their own or working for their own future.

Our older adults are especially lost in a world they don't know with categories that no longer apply and opinions that are considered outdated or even discriminatory in many cases. They knew what they had to do but now that they have attained their goals what do they have left. In the olden days, parents would move back in with their adult children when they could no longer care for themselves. They were of value to the family and respected for their experiences and knowledge but not anymore. The knowledge they hold is no longer of use to them or anyone else.

I find myself battling this reality both on my own behalf as well as with my elderly mother and my adult children. What does this world hold for us, where do we fit in and why does it have to be so hard?

I grew up in the 90's in the last days of generations that have long gone by. We were expected to categorize everything and everyone and fit in our categories and stick to them. Hazing or bullying was a very real part of our adolescence and encouraged those that could, to fit into the "best" categories and if they didn't or couldn't they would feel the ethnocentric behaviors of the groups that thought they were better than them.

Back then we didn't have the depression and suicide rates that we see today. Kids were pissed off or upset but they learned to get over it, in most cases. This definitely caused a lot of mental health issues that have filled therapist's office hours for years and have limited the success and satisfaction of many people as they grew up and moved onto adulthood.

If we go back further to our parents or grandparent's generation, the world was even more harsh. Societies did not have any leeway for those that didn't comply with the norms of society.

Who the Fuck Am I?

Norms were developed based on the requirements of society and what was expected and acceptable behavior in a means to reach an outcome. They had to learn the social expectations of their own gender, age, physical attributes and even mental capabilities and fill those positions in society. They were shunned or pushed out if they did not offer what their society needed.

I feel that compliance is much more difficult in this day and age because the requirements or norms are not set in stone and no one really knows what is expected of them. If they are aware of expectations, they can change them or they can be changed without any notice. People are left struggling to comply, on a day to day basis, with social norms that may be foreign to them or impossible to meet. Families often have a separate set of expectations that may mirror social cues in some ways but may also veer far off from what is expected or acceptable in social settings.

As one that always stood out in my own family and life, I often battle with acceptance. Whether it is in my own head or if others are judging me, I am not sure, but I do hesitate in public or private settings. Sometimes I don't want to participate in social activities because I am not confident that it is right for me or that I am right for the situation.

Our reputation is one way that our place in society is managed for us. The way others view and judge us places a certain stereotype, value or label, that we may or may not agree with but once it is in place we can try our whole lives to get rid of it.

Often times our behaviors in youth and teenage years will earn us a reputation of being the odd one out, the bad guy or some other aspect of negativity in society and we can struggle to earn our way back in without ever attain a true placement with our peer groups. This can be in social or personal settings. Our reputation with our friends and family is often the hardest reputations to make or break.

My family history has shown me that these reputations can lead you on a specific path in your own life and even be passed down to

Who the Fuck Am I?

your children and future generations. When religion was much more mandatory in daily life. An ancestor was likely to hold the title of priest or preacher in their own town or community. It is very common for that career or title to be passed down through several generations. It is less common today but I've found seven generational church leaders and elders in my own ancestry.

If your grandparents were religious folks. They never missed a Sunday session, partook in bible studies and potluck gatherings and never failed to donate their 10% to the church. You may be welcomed into that social organization with open arms. You would also be expected to be just as pious, good hearted and worthy of their affections.

On the other hand, if you were known as a "Hell Raiser" in your youth it may very well be that your children will also be recognized as such. They may be shunned in the family or social groups. Your descendants may even be brought in and harassed by law enforcement, if your reputation was severe enough to warrant it.

Beyond what others think of us lies what we think of ourselves. Taking a subjective angle on our place in our families and societies we can begin to hash out how we feel, think and act towards certain aspects of the social hierarchy. Our physical and mental responses to situations and people also have a strong influence on what categories we believe we fit into.

You may be smart but are you as smart as the others in the group. You may be loving but do you love them as much as they love you or vice versa. Do you feel that this group respects you or shows affection to you as a member? These are all questions that we ask ourselves when trying to figure out where we fit in.

Our emotional responses are extremely valuable and often overlooked or completely ignored in this process as well. When you have justified that you are as smart as the others and they do want you in their group you may feel a rush of endorphins that cause happiness but do those feelings last.

Who the Fuck Am I?

After a while does the new wear off and you begin to feel less than the others or feel embarrassed if you didn't get something right. Do you feel fear that you will be abandon by the group if you do not comply with what is expected of you? Do the others pick on you or purposely engage negative responses from you? Do you feel the need to embarrass or bully them in order to make yourself feel better?

All of these emotional responses are trying to tell you something. If you listen, you can find a better place, a comfortable place where belonging is like second nature. You can fit in without trying but if you continue to struggle, trying to be something or someone that you are not, your mental health will suffer.

There is also the objective viewpoint. Most often used by psychologists, sociologist or anthropologist in studies of human minds, group and cultures. We have this understanding in our everyday interactions as well. We base our opinions of group make up and interactions on our own observation of our surroundings.

Have you ever noticed that someone just didn't belong? They were not like the others in the group they were trying to fit into. You may or may not have been a part of said group. By watching from an unbiased standpoint, you can easily see that there are traits or behaviors that make one individual stand apart from the rest.

Though we struggle with these social norms and every family, city, and country may have very different ideas about norms, we cannot live without them. They are a purely human development and any society trying to function without norms would quickly be over run. The norms of the dominating force would soon take over. We cannot be without organization of some kind in social groups.

Rules, expectations and laws are all forms of social norms. Without them people would do whatever they wanted. This would be hazardous and uncontrollable. In fact, norms are a means to control a group of individuals for the overall benefit of the group. Imagine if there was no rule against violence. People are innately

Who the Fuck Am I?

violent and it would take no time at all to go back to the gladiator times of ancient Rome. We would be solving all of our problems, creating new ones and entertaining the masses with blood sport. Just think about the current obsession with true crime, the bloodier or more bizarre the better.

What if there was no law against theft? Why would anyone work for what they wanted if they could just take it from someone else? Our societies would falter almost immediately. Without people working to create things there would be none. We are already feeling the pain after the pandemic, lack of employees due to death, illness or despair and fear. Shortages of basic products like toilet paper from the same things. Crime rates are skyrocketing because people are suffering and choosing to steal to survive.

Even our expectations about child abuse and neglect are familial and social norms that must be protected or we would see a dramatic rise in those areas. So many children suffer as it is, with rules, expectations and laws to protect them and people still do terrible things. What if, we as a people did not even try to stop them or that from happening.

What kind of world would that be and could you live in it? I know that I could not. Beyond the horrible things people would do without rules, what about the lack of good things we take for granted that people wouldn't do if they didn't have to. Road work, sewer repair, burying the dead, these are all direly important tasks within a community but what if they didn't get done?

Chores like dishes, vacuuming and mowing the lawn are much less important on the life or death scale. Yet, many households are falling apart without these basic tasks being completed. What about raising and managing the children? Whose job is it and why does it have to be done? Does it have to be done? In many situations, today, the answer is no. People are too busy or lazy to care or to even understand the importance of raising our children with morals and beliefs to fit in to the society for which we are a part.

Who the Fuck Am I?

This breakdown is leaving families and societies without respect for each other, our places within our groups and a lack of understanding of who we are or who others are. If no one has a set category or place and those placements are not important how can we be important to the group, to our family or even to ourselves. It is a complete loss of pride and value.

The struggle to find our placement in social groups and the absence of common norms that are enforced throughout those groups are causing the breakdown of societies, as we know them, and the human experience within societies. While norms are intrusive and intense mechanisms of social structure they are in place because we created them.

We needed norms in order for larger social groups to exist and function cohesively without all the violence and crime. We need a place to fit in and call our own in order to be beneficial members of society. In order to understand ourselves and our reason for doing all the things we don't really want to do.

We are all fucked up due to our families, societies and histories. We must also take a percentage of the blame on ourselves for allowing it to be this way. We need to love one and other the best we can and accept the love that is given as imperfect as it is. We have to see past our inadequacies and connect within our families and societies. We can find our place within these groups through judgement, observation and adaptive behaviors but we must fit in, one way or the other, for our own survival as well as our sanity.

END
Part 1.

So, That's

WTF is Wrong with

Me.

Who the Fuck Am I?

Part 2

WTF Makes Me Feel This Way?

My Daughter just wants to grow up and get away from me. In a world that offers so much I guess that's ok. She doesn't need me like she once did. I don't make her feel any sort or kind of way. She can get anything that I have to offer from the internet now anyway.

Our families aren't important anymore. They don't mean what they did back in the day. Your mother may very well love you but you don't need her love in the same way that she needs yours.

We are building generations that depend on strangers online for the emotional and moral support that they need. They avoid in person contact every chance they get. Social interaction is hitting the like button or posting an angry emoji. If mom tries to hug you it's disgusting and out of place.

We both battle depression and anxiety from the missing maternal bond. Society says that is fine, therapy will bridge the divide. Talking is all she really needs. So, you talk and talk and pay all day but there is nothing left for the therapist to say. A venting session, that's all this is, like the ones we used to get each day when we would sit down for dinner. We'd listen to each other and care

Who the Fuck Am I?

what everyone had to say.

When therapy isn't working, you must be beyond repair. We'll medicate away the feelings that are causing your bad day. Those feelings of pain that you must share, they are to blame, weren't you aware?

Therapy and medication are not solutions but treatments for symptoms of the life we lead. The root of your problems is that we are together but all alone too. How can we be happy when we are all together in the same room, aching and hurting, too afraid to share. Looking to our phones for hope and repair.

5

21st Century Societies Do Not Benefit from Meaningful Relationships

"You can talk with someone for years, every day, and still, it won't mean as much as what you can have when you sit in front of someone, not saying a word, yet you feel that person with your heart, you feel like you have known the person for forever." — *C. JoyBell C*

Families don't run farms anymore. A few do but for the most parts kids leave home and families spread apart. Everyone needs their own homes, their own space. Why on Earth would the extended families want to live together, work together and depend completely on each other in this day and age? Everyone can be whatever they want to be, can go wherever they want to go and can do whatever they want to do.

On the farm, kids would have to help their parents with the household chores, cooking, cleaning, repairs and taking care of the family. They would also be expected to help out with basic farmhand chores like milking, cleaning, herding, tilling, planting and sowing, machinery repair and organization.

Who the Fuck Am I?

They would also have to live with each other. Often times Moms and Pops, aunts and uncles, remaining grandparents and all the kids would share one large parcel of land on which they would all live and work. Occasionally, each family unit would have their own home but more times than not they would all share one big farm house. This created even more close quarters and tensions were high all of the time.

They did all of this for survival. There was no great payday. Kids couldn't afford to go out at night or buy nice things for their significant others. That is if they even had time to date. With this strenuous work load, many had to work from dawn until dusk with no time at all for themselves.

The lifestyle of the time didn't have much to offer outside of the home. People were bonded with their families. Their very livelihoods depended upon these bonds. Even when someone pissed you off or you just couldn't stand their annoying behavior, you had no choice. You had to cope with many uncomfortable realities back then.

The 19th and 20th centuries were a great time of industrialization for all nations. Modernization and industrialization called young people away from their families and into the cities to work in factories, shipping yards and delivery jobs. These jobs could pay more and gave the worker the independence from their families they had longed for. They didn't have to comply with the strict regulations and responsibilities that were the norm back at home.

Until this point, people got all of their food locally, straight from the farms. Often times the same family would deliver your milk, eggs and veggies at the same time every week. This built strong bonds within the community and family to family.

These bonds built and grew into a strong bartering society that could count on each other for anything and it often started with the farmers. What does anyone need more than food? Farm families would build working relationships with the butcher that would prepare their meat for sale and in return would receive discounts or free meat for his family. The seamstress would make all of the farmer's overalls and the children's clothes in exchange for fresh milk and eggs. The local teachers would be welcomed into the local's homes for meals in a trade for their educating of the children. The towns people would take care of their teachers in respect for their dedication and the lack of significant personal relationships they would suffer do to their choice of career.

People did use cash and coin for goods in the 19th and 20th centuries. They would still form meaningful relationships within their families and the communities they lived in because they had to. Your life would not be fulfilling and well lived without bonds with everyone else in society. You didn't want to go without any common goods or services because you were a dick to Suzie!

It was natural to build bonds with individuals that you would see or interact with on a daily basis. A smile and nod would turn into asking how the family was, then maybe a shared meal or gathering during the fall harvest. Back then it was much harder to keep goods good for a long period of time, so the people would gather and use a lot of the easily spoiling edibles.

Eventually, these bonds and gathering would grow into marriages and partnerships that would tie the families together for the long term. Communities were strong when each member had the others wellbeing at heart and their survival was of the ultimate interest. People took pride in their relationships and the capabilities of keeping their communities strong and well.

Unfortunately, with ever advancing modernization and digitalization we have lost all that made us strong and connected us to one and other. I don't know who butchers the animals that my family eats. I have no clue where the chickens are raised that lay our eggs. The cow's milk that we drink travels across the country and is being replaced by nut milk. In the long run, it will make no difference what so ever to me or my daily life.

On top of the loss of community and meaningful relationships within them, we've also lost our connection to our food. Which is

Who the Fuck Am I?

creating a nutritional crisis and an obesity dilemma but that is a story for another book and another day.

We have come to a point in human existence that we believe money or wealth is more valuable than human interaction and connection. We grow farther and farther from each other every day and will give up every bond we've shared for millennia just to save a buck or earn a few more.

We choose careers based on how much money we'll make rather than being a jack of all trades. We are no longer capable of taking care of many aspects of our own lives. We require others to do the most menial tasks for us. We buy our food and clothes from strangers. Then go to a job where we package or sell food and clothes to strangers. No meaningful relationships there, where many marriages would have blossomed just a few generations ago. That's okay those marriages may have gotten in the way of our careers anyway.

We spend our hard-earned money on video games and pass times. We can do these at home alone rather than gathering with others. We don't want or need to get to know each other or insert meaning or emotion in our lives.

Our lives have been dwindled down to a number of hours for a set amount of money. We use that money to pay for a life that many of us cannot or do not enjoy anyway. We are lacking the fulfillment of meaningful relationships and the joy that those interactions bring. Bonds within our families are practically nonexistent and we do not build friendships or bonds within our community anymore.

We used to work to live. We'd spend our days and night taking care of each other, our household and our farms for the livelihood of them and the unity that they would bring. Which then nourished our hearts and minds, gave us pride and compassion and kept everyone honest and needed.

Today, we live to work at the cost of all of those things. We have lost our familial commitments as well as the pleasure and passion they brought. We let our children be raised by daycare and elementary schools and our elderly die in homes. We have not the time to care nor be there for them. That loneliness leaves a void that cannot be filled or repaired.

The gaping holes within us stem from the misunderstanding of our evolutionary paths. We're born weak and needy, develop through care and compassion and end our lives needy and weak once more. The transgression through time is the ultimate human trial and we are missing it. Which means we cannot suffer or learn. We cannot grow or feel the true reward of being present with and for our loved ones. That is what it truly means to be human. Life is not about how much money we can save or even share.

While money is the root of all evil and despair, it is what we've lost in its acquisition that will be the true downfall of humanity, our bonds with each other. We no longer need each other for our basic survival. Children are no longer raised by the group. You know that old saying, *it takes a village to raise the children!*

Our elders are not respected and needed for their long-standing knowledge and experience. They are often locked away in nursing homes and forgotten about. Sadly, this causes pain and suffering for them and extenuated struggles for the extended families to which the elders would have been a massive benefit. We don't work for our families and their shared benefit. Our families do not benefit from our work and are slowly falling apart.

6

Modern Family Meltdown

"Everyone has a paradigm that defines his or her reality. This paradigm is created, largely, by society. So, it is limited because it does not include our mind and soul's desires". — *Itayi Garande*

Our societies are defining factors in our development and they are ever changing as are we. No matter how much we want to or how hard we try we cannot maintain a way of life that no longer exists in the communities we live in. The old-fashioned way, the more simplistic versions of family and livelihood have been eliminated and the struggle to grow, develop and fit into this new complex world is ever demanding.

Parents are finding it too difficult to pay the basic household bills and give their kids the modern amenities without both of them working full time jobs. This leaves the kids alone a lot of the time and many of the most important life altering experiences are not shared by the family. Parents are meant to be there for their kids during these developmental times to help them understand and cope with changes in their bodies and minds.

Children are bonding more with friends than their families if they bond with anyone at all. This is when the mental health struggles begin. If left alone and unattended they don't learn to cope with their own emotions. Those emotions will ravage the poor child's mind. Leaving them shy or embarrassed with poor self-esteem and a lack of understanding of social interactions.

Families are melting down, parents are gone all the time and kids are losing that purity that we often attribute to youth. Society is raging on, growing and developing new technologies that will be required to maintain our place within the social structure. The long list of "bills" becomes full of extra necessities that are only important to our social placement and not our survival.

People are working their lives away, giving up their bonds with their families and working themselves to the bone for things that we don't really need but want to fit in. Cable television, cellphones, apps and accessories, designer apparel, expensive cars and apartments are all dedicated to our social class. They do not benefit our well-being and most often harm our relationships further. Our addiction to non-necessary goods is causing the downfall of modern families.

Parents are working longer hours, farther from home just to make an extra buck in attempts to provide more. They are accepting longer commute times and less time for themselves or their families. Households are often cared for by maids or babysitters as are the kids. This does not encourage proper care or strong bonds and everyone in the family feels the loss and pain of the changes.

Sadly, technology has almost convinced us that it is a suitable replacement for our family's love and affection. People have become bonded to their cell phones in an unhealthy way. They are convenient for communication but have developed into a 24/7 accessory for everything. They are used for work and education, collecting photos and memories as well as becoming our only form of social interaction.

Social media has taken over the inner personal relationships and it is costing us our humanity. Humans require face to face communication in order to sense others emotional responses as well as to get a feel for them. Chemical and hormonal cues correlate to our behavior and emotional connection and allow us to know each other in a deeper sense.

People are "catfishing" and building online relationships with others based on a set of values and characteristics that they do not necessarily have. The other side of that is that honest people are building emotional connection with people that do not actually exist. This may not seem too severe but it is causing mental trauma and suffering when the reality of the situation is exposed.

Teens are dating online and not in person. Since Covid, a lot of them are even getting their education completely online. There is absolutely no face-to-face contact or chances to build and tune their senses or judgment centers. These important abilities have evolved with us and been used throughout generation, decades, centuries and even millennia to place ourselves in the best possible situation to pass on our genetic code to future generations.

Young people are satisfying their primal instincts by gratifying themselves with their careers and lifestyles and not choosing to have families. They are not getting married or sharing their lives with each other and definitely not having kids. Who wants to have kids anyway?

Parenting is hard and demanding. You have to put this other life form before yourself or your desire to attain more. A lot of kids in this generation have been raised by television or elementary school teachers and lack the basic familial bonds that led to a desire to pass it on. They have never felt the intense love that a family can and should share. They have no need for families.

Our ancestors needed each other. Their basic survival required partnership and strong bonds. They were dependent on future generation to maintain their livelihoods and survive adulthood and their elder years. Children and grandparents were weak and fragile and they literally needed parents to take care of them on a day-to-day basis. There was no financial reward for this loving care, just the existence and continuation of the family and that was enough back then. Now, it is not.

We are pulling further away from our families and those meaningful bonds. The bonds that used to be developed over our lifetimes and assured us of someone to love and that loved us in return. These relationships were our strongest asset of mental health. Our communication and dependence on each other kept us bonded and sane.

7

Therapy Helps but I'm Still Alone

"Loneliness is my least favorite thing about life. The thing that I'm most worried about is just being alone without anybody to care for or someone who will care for me". — *Anne Hathaway*

Loneliness is a brutal enemy. It waits until you are at your weakest and attacks you, mind, body and soul. Where your family used to be, in these times of weakness and suffering, you are left alone to fend for your own sanity.

Therapy has been developed in this new society as a replacement for meaningful relationships. Basically, you pay someone to play with you. They listen to your fears and concerns, allow you to let it all out. You can bitch and moan, cry or yell, and they will be there as long as you pay.

The sad part is the mind knows that this is not a meaningful relationship. This is a service for cash relationship and as soon as the money runs out your "friend" is gone and you are left alone with your pain and anguish once more.

Human interaction is a rewarding experience as the brain cues the release of hormones and endorphins that equate happiness, joy and blissful feelings. Therapy is not meaningful and therefor does not encourage any of those releases and is not of equal benefit. Yes, you can vent to a person, instead of yourself in a mirror, but you do not get the internal reward of human contact. Our brains beat us out once more.

As we continue to pay to play, we incur further mental damage from lack of human interaction. This further enflames the rage and pain that we feel. Our self-esteem does not get any better and our depression gets worse. Why on earth are we trying so hard in a world that could give a shit whether we live or die?

More problems equal more hours of therapy and more money per hour. The cycle never ends it just gets worse and worse, longer and longer. It doesn't solve our problems. At the end of the day, we must ask; is paying a stranger to play with us really worth our hard-earned money? The money we gave up our families and meaningful relationships to earn. We are paying a stranger to listen and listen alone because they are no replacement for the relationships that have been sacrificed.

Say we do continue to pay. We find a way to make the commitment. Somehow, we come up with the average of $100 per hour for this person to listen to our problems. Only the problems we are aware of and are willing to admit. Probably not the ones we really need to talk about because those are too embarrassing and we are too ashamed to voice them out loud, to a stranger. They still do not begin to address the cycle of problems this entire therapy system is causing.

For instance, the idea that a stranger is listening to all of our deepest darkest secrets and worries or at least the ones we can bring ourselves to talk about, then they are pretending to care! In the back of our heads, we know darn good and well that this person cannot possibly care about every patient they have or every problem every one of those patients has. We are consciously aware of this false dependency.

Who the Fuck Am I?

We are actively participating in pretend relationships and hoping that our brain isn't smart enough to know the difference. It is! Our brain always is smarter than whatever we are trying to trick it. It will release different chemicals in an attempt to make us aware of our circumstances. Our brain always functions for our own protection and survival. For the sake of this new world, we will continue to push our brain back and live in a state of continuous denial. This is unhealthy, unacceptable and unsustainable.

Beyond the mental strain that this places on us it is also a great waste of our time. Time is finite and we each only get so much. How can we possibly spend hours of our lives with people that don't know or care about us or our problems, creating more problems and making ourselves feel worse. It is insanity and that is what we're supposed to be treating.

Looking back to my ancestors has taught me so much about a lack of time. Many were gone in their forties or before. They didn't get a chance to watch their children grow or get married, the ones that lived to adulthood that is. They were thankful for every moment and everyone that they got to spend their short, valuable time with. I wish to be like them. I want to want to be with someone, everyone, my dearest ones.

I need meaningful relationships and I suppose you do too or you probably wouldn't be reading this book. How meaningful can our lives be if we do not truly share them with the people we love. If we do not have people that we love or that love us in return, we are truly alone in this world and no amount of money can change that.

Beyond the historical need to survive and depend on each other, I need human interaction. I need to feel needed. I need someone to call, when I wake up in the morning and nothing is going right. I need them in the evening when I think I heard a sound. I need them in an emergency, when I don't know what to do. I need a shoulder to cry on, one that will give me a hug and hold me dear, one that wants to be there for me and has no reason to care but they do anyway.

Who the Fuck Am I?

It's ok if we are not inseparable or don't even talk to each other every day. I just want to know I'm needed in some form or some way. I know I sound so needy but I believe we all are on the inside. It's just because of society that we shutter and we hide. We don't want to appear weak. We don't want anyone to know that we need them more than they need us. What would we do if people knew how fragile we really are?

The fear of being rejected has taken over our psyche and keeps us from expressing our true loving selves. In many cases, there has been rejection in the past and that deep damage comes back to the surface at the very thought of putting your feelings out there for others to see. This tends to make people mean and grumpy. No one likes to feel insubstantial or easily passed over for someone stronger with much more to hide.

Our lives are meant to be lived together. We create reasons to gather and share. When times get tough or the weather too cold, we plan holidays to spend with the ones we love because we know that is what keeps us going. Sadly, these gatherings have become something to avoid. The judgment or curiosity that we all often share has become a way to shun someone or make them feel some kind of way.

This concept has lent itself to my title as one of the most understood and experienced ailments of our loss of familial bonds and an extreme cause of mental anguish and illness today.

Don't Worry, Your Ancestors Can't Ruin Christmas Dinner is meant to grab your attention and allow you to relate. We have all had that dinner, when an aunt or uncle started trouble, your mother in law put your cooking down, someone didn't want to sit by you or you spend an entire day in great company but none was truly shared. So many get together and spend the day on their phones. The reward is something other than the mental repair we require. It is more damage, more of the same. Our experiences are mostly sad and leaves us dismayed.

The Past is the Best Present for the Present represents our need to get back to our past. By learning and understanding our past we can, in fact, be better in our present situations and circumstances. To see the suffering our ancestors lived through and the way they never gave up we can bring that into the 21st century and apply it to our own problems. To learn of the loss of infants and the elderly so easily and often we can truly appreciate our own families better. By reading the stories of our past and our family's migrations we can be thankful for our stability.

There are so many lessons there to be learned and earned. It is sad that we have lost track of everything that we had. Our lives are left empty and meaningless when just being alive is the most meaningful thing there is. We strive for some sense of perfection that is impossible to attain. We trash ourselves for not meeting the unreasonable expectations that our societies have claimed.

To share this reality of our past with our present families is the greatest accomplishment we could have. To open their minds and hearts to their own past and the ways that it can influence the present could draw us back together.

Spending our therapy sessions with people that share our ancestry can save us hours and money that we could spend exploring our ancestry and feeling the reward of the years that have past and lessons that can be learned.

Sadly, when the store-bought therapy doesn't work, we do not turn to our loved ones, accept them for who they are. Nor do we accept that all of our judgements are human nature. They are the way for us to better and benefit ourselves. They do not require us to abandon each other. Rather we should embrace our differences and hardships and bond over them. Help one and other to cope in this traumatic world we face now.

Instead, we turn to Big Pharma and the drugs we can take to make it all go away. Unfortunately, they do not erase the pain or mental distress that has been caused but they do lead to further mental anguish and physical ailments as well.

8

Medicine Doesn't Fix Lonely

"Addiction is just a way of trying to get at something else. Something bigger. Call it transcendence if you want, but it's a rat in a maze. We all want the same thing. We all have this hole. The thing you want offers relief, but it's a trap." – *Tess Callahan*

I want to start this chapter by saying that modern medicine is a life saver in many ways. I understand that a lot of people cannot function in their everyday lives without some type of mood altering or stabilizing medicines. The Zoloft and Xanax prescriptions allow people to function within their mental illness. It keeps them from giving up and giving in to the self-hate and sabotage.

Sadly, medicine doesn't fix lonely though. Individuals are trying to fix a social problem all by themselves. We are taking every pill under the sun to fill the voids and try to feel better but we are still alone. That is where another issue arises. Self-analysis that leads to self-hate.

You may share some of your symptoms or feelings with a doctor to get that prescription but there is plenty that you do not reveal because it's embarrassing or you don't think it's important.

Who the Fuck Am I?

That leaves you to judge yourself and we all know that we are our own worst critics.

Taking medicine and living a solitary life often sends us inwards and that can be more damaging and extremely painful. We focus on our flaws and feel every difference deeply. Our hearts can be broken without us even realizing that we are at risk. We only think of broken hearts when you're in love or falling out of it, dating or getting dumped, it always requires another person that carelessly crushes your most essential organ.

I would argue that we break our own hearts more often and severely than anyone else ever could. Our brutal critiques of our own worth and capabilities can be more destructive and real than anything anyone else can think about us or say to us. We are in our own heads and believe the illusion that we tell to ourselves.

If you believe that you are not good enough to fit into society than you will not behave good enough or try to put yourself out there. If you believe that your flaws are more significant than your assets than you will not try to accomplish your desires or goals. If you believe that you are crazy, then you will fill that stereotype in your own mind. You will accept that no one else would ever want to deal with that craziness.

Medication may calm your anxiety or make it easier to close yourself up in your house without completely losing it but it does not fix the loneliness or empty feelings that you hold inside. We're left questioning what is actually inside of us. What are we bottling ourselves up with? Are we crazy or insane? Will the medicine help us be normal? Do we have what it takes to fit into society? Do we have a good sense of humor? Do we fall to dark humor too much? Can we be good friends with others? Are our families right about us? Are we losers? Are we annoying?

All of these thoughts and many more circle in our cranium, daunting us and luring us to self-hate or self-pity. If we are medicated enough to eliminate those thoughts and feelings the medication definitely impedes on our ability to lead a fulfilling life.

Who the Fuck Am I?

That is the burden of medicating away our mentalities. We may not feel the bad or difficult emotions but we cannot feel the good or rewarding emotions either. How can things get better if we cannot enjoy our existence in anyway? We have to worry about whether the medicine will make us feel better or worse.

Antidepressants and depressants, antipsychotics, mood stabilizers, anxiolytics and stimulants are all types of drugs prescribed for different mental health diagnosis. They all come with higher or lower risk factors of certain side effects. Headaches, weight gain, dizziness, dry mouth, muscle spasms and cramps, nausea, loss of sex drive, constipation and sleepiness or problems sleeping are all common side effects of each of these drugs to one extent or another.

We are left wondering if medicating the anxiety from going outside is worth this pounding headache and gaining twenty pounds in three weeks. Do we want to sleep all day long and lose our romantic desires for a balanced mentality instead of the highs and lows of bipolar disorder? Really good questions but there are no in-betweens. Either you take the meds or you don't and you alone deal with the consequences.

That was just a list of the clinically recognized side effects. Many people experience a wide range of unrecognized effects as well. These are the side effects that leave many mentally ill people un-medicated because they do not accept these feelings from the pills.

This is a very common complaint in rehab centers, psych wards, and even jails or prisons. People simply do not feel like themselves. They don't recognize themselves in the mirror. They cannot understand their own emotions or lack thereof and cannot sustain a desire to live like that. They cannot control their own behaviors with or without the medication.

It is often too difficult trying to medicate away the person you are naturally. You cannot understand who you are becoming. You attempt to find your place in this world or create a place for yourself with in the hierarchy of society. People fail all the time. They give up and end up suicidal or worse.

Unfortunately, the medicine isn't meant to make you normal or fit in. It's meant to keep you from causing a scene or disrupting the status quo. Society must go on no matter how you feel.

Our ancestors didn't have the opportunities to treat mental illness as we do today. They had to choose if it was bad enough that it had to be dealt with and this was a serious if. If you were mentally ill and the doctor couldn't figure out how to "fix" you it often meant a life sentence in an insane asylum. Many children would be placed in these homes for their entire lives, if their parents couldn't deal with any abnormal behavior.

By 1940, a Portuguese neurologist named António Egas Moniz won a Nobel Prize for his invention of the, well-known and immensely feared, lobotomy. A surgery that was performed on many mentally ill patients and then people with any condition, it seemed, that severed the ties of the frontal cortex of the brain leading to an end of many symptoms.

Unfortunately, for many patients receiving this surgery, it did not necessarily solve their problems, if they had any to begin with but it did leave them carefree and docile. Which meant they were easier to manage by their families and society as a whole. There were often much worse side effects from the surgery than the patient previously suffered. These were ignored for the benefit of society.

Mental health issues have been a serious problem for individuals, families and society forever and have been dealt with in a variety of ways. Ways that never truly solved the base issues. Modern attempts with therapy or medication have a range of success depending on the situation or circumstances but neither actually address the cause of the illnesses. The side effects of these treatments may very well leave the person in a worse scenario then when they got started. A look back in time shows that we are all so lucky to have semi-beneficial acceptable mean of treatment today rather than lobotomies or life in a psych ward that our ancestors faced.

Medication is useful but it isn't perfect and it doesn't fix everything. The damage we all face due to our modern societies and our lack of connection is astounding. We need to rebuild our families and find meaningful connections in order to address the sadness and loneliness that we all face. Our ancestors can show us how if we look back and learn from their experiences.

END
Part 2.

So, That's

WTF Makes Me Feel

This Way.

Part 3

WTF Can I Do About It?

I try to focus my energy and enjoy a new hobby or two. Most of them are pointless and don't take my mind off of the stress, sadness or loneliness I feel. I've found a new passion that takes it all away but interestingly enough it brings my family back to me. I'm sure that sounds confusing or even a bit insane but it is true and I will tell you what it is.

Ancestry research is the pastime for me. It's easy to get into and a pleasure to embrace too. I can lose myself for hours and find myself too. Sometimes, I like to go back and track as many generations as possible to find out where it all began. Other times it's fun to look up school yearbook photos or marriage records for the family that I know currently.

Somewhere in between, I've found lost ancestors and links to royalty. Not that it really matters but it's interesting to me. I love to make connection with people far away. People that have no obvious bond with me or this life that I have to lead.

Who the Fuck Am I?

My immediate family want nothing to do with me but when I travel back in time it's a different world I see. Families that depended on each other. Bonds that couldn't be broken even when one crossed the great sea.

My ancestors immigrated from places I have never seen. They come from Norway, Germany and France, all to the American continent. The new world as it once was known. Known for its freedom from hypocrisy and persecution. A land for everyone to start a new. They could bring their cultures and customs and build a nation that we all can share.

I felt like my life had always been here but now I see that my genes have come from everywhere. They have traveled over miles and through millennia. It is a privilege to carry my ancestors' traits and skills into this new world that wouldn't even exists if they hadn't fought so hard to give it to me.

Today, I feel like my life is hard, my emotions and mental health make it this way. Historically speaking we're really doing fine. If only we could make connections that save these maternal bonds and enforce are matrilineal line. Then we'd have it all figured out and we could enjoy it too.

Our families are all that really matter. Their love is all that binds us   to   each   other   through   out   space   and   time.

9

Mental Movement Keeps You from Self Hate

"If we allow our 'high creativity' to remain alive, we will never be bored. We can pray, standing in line at the super market. Or we can be lost in awe at all the people around us, their lives full of glory and tragedy, and suddenly we will have the beginnings of a painting, a story, a song." *-Madeleine L'Engle*

Sometimes are brains need rest and other times they need preoccupation. When our minds are left idle, we falter to the same old feelings and thoughts of inadequacy and failure. We must learn to keep our thoughts under control if we want to keep our mental health in check.

Mental Movement refers to anything that keeps your mind from wondering. As mentioned in the quote for this chapter, it could be prayer, judgement or relating to someone we envy, it could be research or study, even companionship. Anything that gets your mind focused.

One thing that I've learned is beneficial in practicing focus, after leading a life plagued by depression or anxiety, is that we have plenty of extra emotion, tension and pressure to put into our focus. Take all of that stuff that you've been blocking out or hiding from and bring it to the forefront of your mind. Put that energy into your pleasure instead of your pain.

Through consistent effort you will feel your mind being drawn to the subject or item that you have been focusing it on and drifting further from the thoughts and worries that have brought you pain.

You can allow yourself to follow the focal point that your mind chooses. There are many avenues that you can let yourself get lost in, all of which are therapeutic and purifying. By allowing your mind to guide itself down healthy paths it will inevitably find less time to ponder poor decisions or regrettable events. Leaving you feeling better or feeling less, whichever is your goal.

When I chose to do my DNA test, I had specific questions in mind but that is not always the case. I had been told stories that were not accurate and many details of my lineage were forgotten or hidden with purpose. My immediate family were not close and were not strong. We all had issues and broken bonds.

When I began to look back at my ancestry I was struck with wonder and awe. I held wonder for every detail of the stories that I'd never been told. Wonder for my ancestors who had suffered so tremendously yet survived and we didn't even know about them. My mind was filled with awe for the way that many of my ancestors survived a world that literally wanted to kill them.

When you delve into your ancestry, I guarantee that you will find several lines of interest to you. Someone that lived where you would like to live. Someone that had the strength that you wished you had. A life led for freedom rather than being secluded no matter the consequence. So many lives fought for our freedom and won. So many fought and lost.

It's easy to get carried away, back in time, to another story or another place. Allow your ancestors to guide you to the lessons that resonate with you. Let them show you the bonds that they shared not because they were easy or always satisfactory but because they were required and absolutely necessary for survival.

See the birth and death records going back as far as they were kept, question the probates and wills that were our ancestors lives and deaths.

Today, kids can't wait for their parents to die, hoping for some great payoff, the vacation property in Florida or a cabin in Wisconsin. The money, oh how badly they want the money, assuming that it will make them complete but it won't. Money can never fill the holes inside our souls. The holes that are left from lacking meaningful relationships with our families, especially when the families are gone.

See how all of a man's worldly possessions were divided up between his sons and daughter and finally his wife. Back then women only had the possessions her husband left her. Often times, the sons would be granted the land and business ventures. The daughters that were not married would be granted much of the money left to the estate for survival and dowry. Finally, the widow would remain in the shared home and have a meager number of belongings to live out her days.

The sons would then be expected to care for and provide for their mother as long as she may live. If there were no sons the widow would have to move in with her daughter's families or back in with someone in her maiden family. Tragic really, that an entire life can be eliminated, so quickly, based not only on their own death but on the loss of the spouse.

You can also see trials and tribulations that led to success and growth that were unknown in those days. Villages popping up in places forests had always stood. The first stone school house and the efforts to find and maintain a teacher for the schools. Which was quite a feat, you should look into it sometime.

No matter who your family was or what your personal interests are they are there in your DNA and your Family Tree waiting to be discovered and brought into the future. There are lessons to be

Who the Fuck Am I?

learned and fights that cannot be forgotten. Our ancestors lived through their own times and found the means to survive so that we could be born into a new world. Everything we now hold we owe to them and their suffering, hard work, loss and determination.

It is truly fascinating to compare the things we let bother us today to the things our ancestors were thankful for back then. Everything is relative to our circumstances and the sooner we realize that we create our own terms the better off we will be.

We choose the outline of our life, our jobs, our homes, our pass times. We choose who we spend our time with and how much value we place on our happiness and theirs. We also choose what we stress over and how we deal with that as well.

Today, I have to clean the bathroom. I despise scrubbing the toilet and bathtub. It's a pain sweeping and mopping the floor and washing all the throw rugs. I almost let it bring me down but then I think about my ancestors using corncobs to wipe their behinds in a freezing cold outhouse and I view my struggles differently.

I worry everyday about making rent and paying all the bills. How will I ever afford it all especially with this crazy inflation and our finances crashing into the mud. The internet and cable, the cell phones and app subscriptions, credit cards and timeshare payments, insurances and all. There is so much coming out every day. I know there has to be a better way.

Then, I look back a few generations and learn that my great grandfather built the family cabin with his own two hands. He and my great grandmother raised 11 children in a room no bigger than my living room. No bedrooms to share all the kids grew up sleeping on the floor. The only heat they had was a wood burning stove that had to be packed every morning and night or they would all freeze.

These tiny tidbits and trails have led me through a magnificent discovery of all the things that have brought me here. The people and places that have made my family who and what we are. The struggles that have made difficult decisions necessary. The trauma that has left people unable to care for others or even for themselves.

I have discovered loss that was average and normal for the times that would have had me shook to my core. I have also learned about the type of loss that even my ancestors couldn't bare. I've found family units that were shattered at no fault of their own. There have been extended families that were scattered to the wind and find themselves living at the four corners of the country due to loss and despair.

I have found my path, my people and it is rewarding every single day. To connect with them and appreciate their plight is meaningful. It is extremely beneficial, to me, to have the comparison and the continuation of their stories and their suffering to add to my own.

I have found that I view things differently, when I truly understand, that my life may be difficult but it really ain't that bad. It could always be worse. It probably should be worse. As long as I am thankful for this life my ancestors gave to me. I can find peace in living it no matter what that means.

Today, I am capable of choosing what I learn, how I earn and who I yearn to be. I can include or dismiss anything that is not suitable for me. That was not the case for my ancestors and I must appreciate this opportunity. I live in a time when anything is possible, survival is normal and losses are few and far between, excluding Covid-19.

I live not only for me or my immediate family but I live for them. I live for the children that were lost, the women who never got off the birthing bed. I live for all of the parents that suffered so their children could go on. I live for and through my ancestors and they are a bigger part of me than anyone else can be.

I surround myself in their history and the mysteries that I have yet to figure out. Every day is better now because I can bring them

Who the Fuck Am I?

with me. I am never truly alone for as long as I hold on to their memory they are with me.

Whenever I get a depressing thought, I can relate it to a person from my past that has dealt with the same thing or worse and come out on top. On top of the situation, on top of their own mentality and on top of the world, where I would like to be.

You too can find yourself on top of the world. It's a choice you see. By learning and exploring your own ancestry you can choose who you want to be and how that will affect your day-to-day life.

Choose your family and let them be there for you when your immediate family may not be. Take their accomplishments as reassurance that you too can find a way, the way, to being the person you wish to be and living the life you want to lead.

Ancestry research and discovering your DNA began as mental movement. A way to keep you from going insane inside your head. Along the way, it became more. It opens windows into your heart. It allows you to connect with historic versions of yourself. Your DNA has come a long way from the times and places your ancestors once lived. It's travelled all the way to you, now, and must go on into the future too. Now that you have found your family you may consider yourself found too.

10

Find the Family that Feels Right

"I don't know half of you half as well as I should like; and I like less than half of you half as well as you deserve." — *J.R.R. Tolkien*

The journey has begun and you are starting to have fun. When you wake up in the morning you are curious what interesting details you will find today instead of dreading what came yesterday. You have several lineages that interest you and you have to make a conscious decision which one you want to spend more time researching.

You can choose to dig deeper into recent generations. You can find birth and death records as well as marriage licenses and other legal documents, quite easily for anyone that is deceased. Most of these documents are available for free access and are published on ancestry.com and similar sites.

Newspapers.com also has tons of articles and tidbits online that have been listed in hundreds of thousands of newspapers around the world over the years. You can find wedding announcements and birth announcements, anniversary notices and celebratory articles of many kinds.

Who the Fuck Am I?

Along with all the great information you can find online, there is also a paper trail of terrible events that have been documented throughout history. Crime and tragedy have long been noted as public service announcements as well as sales pitches. Accidents, murders and mysteries fill pages and vaults, all you have to do is have the desire to look.

There are rabbit holes of all kinds and they are wonderful to find. They keep you digging and researching for hours or even days. You never really know what you will find. Sometimes you expect one thing and get something completely different. Other times you don't even know that there was a mystery to find until you get there and the wondering begins.

You can also track lines, as I like to do. Follow your parents back to their parents and their parents and their parents etc. etc. until you cannot go back any further. It's not about the specific detail but more about following the genetics back to different lands. It's about finding the root of your own genetic codes.

Most of us, here in the USA, did not come from here. Indigenous peoples make up just 2% of the overall population. That means that the rest of us have a path to find. These paths could lead us back to England and stop there or many migrated between European countries before coming to the new world.

Scotland, Ireland, Norway and Germany are but a few locations that my ancestors have migrated from. They came here for many reasons and under many circumstances. Each and every one is a distinct day of discovery and usually much longer. I have been researching my ancestry for over 5 years now and still am amazed by discoveries every time I log in!

DNA has connected me with them and I am now able to develop those relationships and figure out why they left their homelands. How they lived and died. When they lived and what their lives were like. I get lost in the societies that existed, the cultures that thrived and the way that I can bring those heritage lines to life in my life.

There is also the elephant in the room, that no one likes to talk about, but it is a definer for many. The Trans-Atlantic slave trade brought hundreds of thousands of men, women and children from countries across Africa to North and South America as well as the Bahamas. Previously, slaves were scattered across Europe. In many cases, it is difficult to find any real documentation of slaves that were transported, but it is definitely a worthy effort to address. Every day we find new records, documents, stories or tales that tell of the lives of these peoples and their captors. It is of utmost importance to give these people a voice, a life, and our remembrance.

Through DNA you can definitely connect with the families of these missing generations and track forward and backwards to make it all line up. There will often be specifics lacking but the basic line is there to find. As are generations of families that have been lost through time and can only be replaced through this valuable genetic research and time connecting all the dots.

These are just a few of the rabbit holes, or lines of inquiry that you may find yourself or, more so, lose yourself in discovering. I assure you that you will find your own trails to follow and histories to discover and they will cross and wind in ways that you have never expected.

Your lineages and migrations will not be the same as mine or many other people's either. There are very few that came from the same places and made the same journeys and survived the same trials that could lead their descendants to the same outcome. You may share a piece or a part of your heritage and that is where the connections lie. As you learn about each one of your ancestors and their independent stories you can begin to paint the full picture of you. You are the product of all of those stories and histories combined. Everyone's story is their own and you can claim that for yourself.

Who the Fuck Am I?

Let's not get ahead of ourselves though. We must start small, with one ancestor or family line. Find one that really speaks to you. Perhaps you always loved French culture and learned to speak the language. Now you find that you have a French ancestor and are really curious about them. Maybe It was a Scot and you loved watching outlander. You just can't wait to find your ancestor that would have been alive at that time and existed through those events.

Whatever the case may be, choose one and let the research begin. As you are going back, you can document as much or as little information about each ancestor as far back as you'd like as long as it is available.

This is where missing links may come into play. All you can do is the best you can do and do not let yourself get frustrated by any lost or missing information. It may come to you in time or you may have to accept that the past was not always the best time for record keeping.

I have been stumped by missing links as recent as 2 generations back and as far back as 12, 13, or even 14 generations back. Sometimes the trails just stop and no matter what I do or how much I look up or call around I cannot go any further. That is just something that I've learned to deal with. However, there is always another line, another member, another life that I can jump to and research them instead.

There is also missing information and that can be a pain even in modern times. We think that we have everything written down, stored well or even online these days. I have requested death certificates that are mysteriously unavailable. Military records are often transported around for different reasons and are lost when you go to claim them. Even birth and death records, just a few generations back, have been lost in fires or floods and can never be recovered.

Who the Fuck Am I?

That is the tragic reality of our human mentality. We are obsessed with keeping records but nature has other plans. Today's record keeping is much safer, for how long I am not sure, but I do know that I personally have 2, 3 or even 4 copies of everything. Paper copies, copies saved to my computer or external hard drive and copies saved to the cloud, as well, as records that are saved to websites such as ancestry, family search, family tree finder, etc. This final method is one of my favorites because it allows all of my effort to be shared with my family, near and far and the public for their own research projects.

Now, that the information is coming together you can put it into your own organization, share it and store it for future generations You can take time to compare and relate to your ancestors. How are you alike and different from them? What makes your life more difficult or easier than theirs?

Obviously, your situation is going to be much different than most of your ancestors. Think of the basics like where you live. Is it warm or cold and how would that affect people in years gone by and how does it affect you? Think of your livelihood, how much different is it for you to make a living than it was for them and what did that include? How about relationships. Do you have one, would you have if you lived back then? What were the quality and meaning behind relationships in this time period or society?

There are many details of modern life that wouldn't have existed even a few generations back and things only got simpler the further you go back. We can both be thankful for these conveniences and be saddened by the burden of trying to keep up with unnecessary necessities. Just the experiment of comparison can make you look at your life in an entirely different light and to be thankful for the day.

Beyond the basics, we can interpret the mental and emotional characteristics of the time. How important was mental health? Were people encouraged to hold or hide emotion? Would you judge yourself the same way through their standards? Would you rather

Who the Fuck Am I?

be held to their standards? Would life be more difficult or easier if you lived in this time period or society?

Our ancestors had all of the same human instincts, emotions and feelings that we do today. The only difference is how their society taught them to cope with the circumstances of the time. Every generation is taught to utilize human characteristics that are beneficial to them and their lifestyles or at least the lifestyle that society wants to encourage.

We are at a time, in the world, that those options are limitless. Societies are incapable of telling everyone how they should think and what they should feel and how they should react to the circumstances of our societies and existence. Therefore, we are left feeling burdened and alone in our suffering but we are not alone.

Our extended families go back farther than we can research or ever know. They have seen, done and been everything we have to, now. We just need to embrace them and the understanding of their lives to benefit from all that they have experienced and accomplished throughout history.

When our significant other isn't so significant or our immediate families don't want us around, we can always reach back in time and claim the family that brought us to this time. You are not alone. Your great grandmother that survived the great depression, she is with you. Her strength will fulfill you. Your great, great uncle that fought in WWI is with you. The things he has seen would bring you to your knees. His strength will embolden you. You are not alone. We are never truly alone. Our ancestors live with us, in our DNA and our ability to survive and live the life that they have given us.

We may feel like we are wondering through the world without a place of our own. We may believe that we belong nowhere, to no people and no community but we are wrong.

We do belong to our family, to our ancestors and to ourselves. Our ancestors didn't fight the battles they won or live through the misery that came for them for us to give up. They survived and sacrificed so that their DNA would live on, would grow and evolve and become you and me. They died so that we could live.

How could we let them down by giving up or letting go of this life we have? We cannot, we will not. We are their legacy and shall suffice to live on in our own glory. We are the fruit that has flourished from our family tree. The sweet nectar of our lives feeding the societies around us.

We will learn and understand the roots, trunk and branches of our tree so that one day we can become them. We can pass our knowledge on and our strength will become the strength of our descendants. Our tree shall tower over the Earth, strong and durable, ready and able to survive all that will come for it. Glad that we have the awareness and understanding of what has been given and what we must give to make our lives meaningful.

We have found our family, found our place in the line of our ancestry and we can now truly appreciate each one of our ancestors for who they were and what they passed down to us.

11

My Ancestors are Awesome

"Happiness is having a large, loving, caring, close-knit family in another city." — *George Burns*

Another city or another time as long as you aren't driving each other crazy or getting on each other's last nerve. They say that distance makes the heart grow fonder, that definitely includes time!

My modern family is not all that close. We all have problems and attitudes that are just not conducive to interaction. We are all living in this modern world where we don't need anyone or anything and it has torn us apart.

Through my ancestry research I have learned that my family tree is full of amazing humans. My ancestors are an inspiration to me and I admire them for their strength, passion, dedication and determination to their families, lives and futures, even if they wouldn't be there to see it.

We all, here in America, have pioneers, puritans and even Quaker ancestors that fled from England and the Catholic church or the protestant revolution. They had beliefs that they would not sacrifice. They had ideas about what life should be and how one should live it and were not willing to change that to stay where they were.

They picked up and left their homes and families, sometimes on very short notice, leaving almost everything behind. Not knowing if they would ever see or hear from their families again but knowing that they must move on to ensure the future of their families and genetic code.

These tenacious people are the very same ones that started many states and cities that we call home today. They came to a new world, a harsh land, a place where they knew nothing and started a new. That is inspirational.

I traced my mother's side of the family back as far as I could. I found many farmers and southern country men. Civil war heroes and men that were on the other side. Eventually, the nameless gave way to a family of daughters. The eldest of which was named Dolly Payne and she grew up to marry a man by the name of James Madison. The very same man that would become the 4th president of the United States of America.

Dolly would go down in history as the first, first lady to dedicate herself to her husband's career as president. She threw great parties and hosted dinners. All the local politicians would attend. She lived her life in a way that led future president's wives to be First Ladies and not just wives. That is inspirational.

My DNA suggested close ties to Norway and upon further research I found that my second great grandfather, also on my mother's side, was in fact from Norway. His life was hard and there wasn't enough farmable land for the population as it was, let alone for it to grow. He chose to leave and come to the new world.

He immigrated here with many men, set to make a life in this new world. They received land grants from the government and settled in Wisconsin. They were foresters and loggers, cutting through the old growth making way for farms and fields. Tragically,

Who the Fuck Am I?

they had run ins with the indigenous peoples that made their homes in the wood and sadly my ancestors won.

These Norwegians built a village and named it Eidsvold after a village from their homeland. They lived together in long houses with communal out houses and an outdoor kitchen. There were only a few men that spoke English and they were communicators and set up work. The others stayed to themselves and spoke in their native tongue. This made starting a family difficult if not impossible, but that is what they came here for. It took them several years before they were able to invite wives from back home and truly feel the reward for all that they had suffered and all that they had given up or lost along the way. That is inspirational.

These immigrants gave up everything that they had ever known. Their culture and customs, left behind, only remembrance and vague attempts to foster them in this new world. America is a mixing pot of all of our ancestor's beliefs and characteristics. Some bits of their culture have survived their travels and time. In a transformed way, they exist to this day. Their religions have been bastardized and their families have been scattered but they made it.

They left their homelands for many reasons. Religious persecution, famine and disease are the most common but lack of land and economic distress weren't far behind. They came across the great ocean, risking life and limb for a chance to live their lives in ways that they saw fit. They came for religious freedom even if it wasn't what they had previously known. They needed land even if they had to fight for it and work their butts off to make it useable.

Many immigrants had to hit the ground running. Starting off in New York where they were shuffled into factories to make a living for their families. The conditions were horrible and unsafe and they worked long strenuous hours for little pay and minimal rewards. They did it though. Our ancestors were tough as nails with dedication and determination to survive.

Who the Fuck Am I?

These men and women showed exceptional character in the face of tremendous challenges. They did not allow the difficulties to slow their progress. They had no choice but to succeed and that was what they would do. They would run those factories until they could do something better. They would clear all the land they needed to grow crops to feed their families and sell for profit. They would use the skills they'd learned from their own land to work for others and prepare they're land for profits as well.

Many immigrants would stay in groups from their countries and work together to create Norwegian, Dutch or Irish villages that share the characteristics of their homeland. It would give them strength and comfort to be among familiarity and it would allow them to share a bit of who they were with each other and pass it on to future generations.

Our Ancestors would make themselves useful in all aspects of society from street sweepers to street light lighters, seamstresses and launders, drivers and walkers, messengers and any other small job that they could do. Societies required skilled laborers as well as odds and ends job attendants and immigrants would fill them all.

The jobs our ancestors completed, out of necessity, often became their livelihood and future careers in the new world. They would be known among society for the jobs they could do and how well they would do them. This aided them as well as their communities in economic development and growth.

Side jobs would become back yard shops, garages or offices and eventually businesses, legal and legitimate. These businesses could then be passed from generation to generation and the skills would be taught through the family. Lives were built, men were made and families were developed and devoted to.

Now-a-days, it's sad to see that we are lacking our exceptional characteristics. Those that our ancestors struggled so hard to provide. Our families are falling apart and our lives aren't valuable even to us. Today, we say it's too hard or it will take too long, I don't want to or I can't. As if our lives weren't meant to be lived just easily survived.

We can look back in time to the real survivalists and we will find that what we are doing isn't a way for us to survive. Our technology and our modern ways have made everyone lazy and willing to die. We've lost our meaning and the value we placed inside. The necessity or need for us to be anything at all or to work for our lives has disappeared.

Our ancestors stood tall and strong when they left their homes and families. They stood through the pain and the fear of what was to come. They stood when everything looked too difficult to bear. When they had lost everything, alone in a new land, they stood their ground and made their own way. Something we have difficulty with today, in the land of our birth, the world we have known, societies that have coddled us and made us so weak.

We need to find our history and where we come from if we hope to pass our lives on to the future. We should cherish the characteristics that made our ancestors strong. The strength that brought them from faraway lands. Through the difficulties of their times, they prospered not merely survived. We need to know from where we grow and who it is that we should follow.

12

How Far We've Come

"No self is of itself alone. It has a long chain of intellectual ancestors. The "I" is chained to ancestry by many factors... This is not mere allegory, but an eternal memory." — *Erwin Schrödinger*

We think that life is hard now but we don't realize that a few generations ago, everything wanted to kill us. It wasn't about finding our happiness or fulfilling our souls. Our ancestors struggled, every day in every way, just to survive.

The very Earth our ancestors lived on was abundant with viruses and bacteria that no one understood for the most part of our history. Illness and disease were a part of everyday life as far back as we have recorded histories and most likely before.

We've all heard of The Black Death, which was caused by a strain of the Bubonic Plague. This disease ravaged the world of our ancestors. Europe, Asia and even Northern Africa lost somewhere between 75 and 200 million persons in the mid-14th century. There was and still is no cure and no methods of care could ease the pain.

Who the Fuck Am I?

Victims and their families would be closed off in their homes to die, usually within 3 days of the first symptoms. This was the only way our ancestors could slow the spread of this horrific killer.

Though the most well-known, this was not the first and would not be the last epidemic of the plague to massacre millions. Way back in the 6th century, the Plague of Justinian had already taken 15-100 million people. The bubonic plague still makes its presence known every few centuries.

In the 17th century the plague hit Italy. In the 18th century it was in Persia. Only a couple million died in each of these smaller waves of the plague but it was still the loss of a couple million lives.

In the mid-19th and 20th centuries, the plague hit hard again. The Third Plague Pandemic, as it is known, started in China and spread quickly throughout Asia killing at least 12 million people and made its way to every inhabited continent through oceanic trade and travel. While this was known as the last great pandemic of bubonic plague it has surged in waves, lessening its victim rate each year into modern times.

We all know and fear the bubonic plague but there have been several equally devastating diseases that have made their way through the ancient and even more recent world. They have taken their toll on our ancestors, family lines, communities and countries as we've grown into the world that we experience today.

Influenza or the flu as we call it today has taken many people to their final resting place. The 16th century was the first absolute pandemic of influenza, in the same regions of the world, Europe, Asia and Africa. Before this, many instances of possible influenza cases and pandemics stem back to ancient Greece and the earliest to 6000 BC in China. These cannot be concluded to have been due to the influenza virus because of a lack in scientific understanding at the time. But it definitely shows that humans have been suffering and dying from the illness for a very long time.

Who the Fuck Am I?

Influenza has a good survival rate compared to the plague but also has the capability to kill many, slow progress and trade and bring societies to their knees. This easily transmittable sickness causes many unbearable symptoms and can kill the weak, children and elderly fairly quickly, leaving families broken and morning.

Small-pox was a terrible disease that killed millions and was likely the decimation of the Indigenous American peoples when Europeans brought the disease across the ocean and they had zero tolerance to it. Luckily for us, the World Health Organization confirmed the last case of Small-pox in the world, back in 1977. Small-pox has officially become the first human disease to be completely eradicated from existence.

This was no small feat but generations and even millennia in the making. The first suspected cases of small-pox were mentioned in mummies of ancient Egypt about 1500 BC. It spread, killing millions throughout Europe and eventually the entire world.

Small-pox raged, the world over, leading to the first inoculations in China in the 16th century. These same methods were adopted in Europe in the 18th century. These inoculations did not do enough to curb the disease and finally, at the cusp of the 19th century, an Englishman named Edward Jenner developed the modern vaccine for the disease. This was the beginning of the end of small-pox.

Beyond these familiar and devastating illnesses, there is a long list of other sicknesses that our ancestors caught, fought, recovered from and died from as a part of their everyday lives throughout the centuries.

Measles and Mumps are probably familiar to you as one of the vaccines our children still require for safety and to attend public schools. There have been a few outbreaks of the measles in recent years. Often starting among the anti-vaxxer communities and spreading even to vaccinated children.

Cholera, Typhoid, Diphtheria, Polio, Whooping Cough, Scarlet Fever, Yellow Fever and Rubella are all known killers. They all easily take the infants and elderly, first and foremost, but can decimate middle aged populations as well and have been known to do so. The invention of modern vaccines has led to most of these conditions disappearing or being controlled for the most part.

Third world countries, such as Africa and parts of south America still have wide spread pandemic rates of some illness. This is due to less industrialized civilizations and less medical interventions. Leading necessary vaccines not to be easily accessible. Many of the world's richest countries and philanthropists have made consistent efforts to aid in vaccine dispersion and disease control around the globe.

Our ancestors had to accept the reality that their lives were not guaranteed and they could take ill themselves or lose family members at any time due to these diseases. They had to be strong and go on anyway. They had to build tolerances to the illness they could, survive the diseases that were possible and develop vaccines and medications to treat the weaker of the population. All of these together have allowed our populations to grow for generations and have allowed the development of technology and the modern societies that we now know.

If people were lucky enough to live until adulthood or even their adolescence and teenage years, it was common practice for families to arrange marriages early. Not necessarily for the boys but girls were to be wed as soon as they were, biologically, ready. This would assure their husband would receive the best of their child bearing years and have the best chance for many children to help support the family and eventually take over the estates.

Unfortunately, especially for the youngest brides, childbirth was also a killer. In the 17th century, it is estimated that women had a 1-2 % chance of dying every time they went into labor. That means that for every one hundred children born one or two of their mothers would die. One century ago, that rate was down to about 600 per 100,000 live births or 6 per 1000, just over ½ a percent! Today, it is at 15 deaths per 100,000 live births, .15 per 1,000 or

.o15% It is truly amazing what all of our modern advancements have allowed.

(Data was researched by Laura Helmuth and can be found at www.slate.com)

Even worse than that the child would die, before the age of one year, approximately 25% of the time and before the age of 15, 45% of the time. This distressing average for child mortality rates dates back not only a few hundred years but a couple thousand to approximately 500 BC. From ancient Rome to Mexico and Sweden infant mortality fluctuated between 35%-60% and stuck at those rates for almost 2000 years before finally declining in the 17th and 18th centuries. These rates have steadily declined until current, with infant mortality rates averaging 4.6%. Some of the wealthiest nations with the highest rated health care, like Iceland, are at a mere .03% and the nations that struggles the most in Africa still see a rate of 14.6%.

(Data was gathered from research done by Our World in Data and can be found at www.ourworldindata.org)

The final measure of basic survival, after disease and illness was life expectancy. There are two methods of estimating life expectancy, the estimate at birth and that after a person had reached 15 years old. Factoring out infant and childhood mortality as well as any pre-existing conditions and post traumatic disabilities from childhood illness that would have taken their toll by the age of fifteen.

Life expectancy increased significantly and consistently from the mid-20th century until modern times. Around 1950 humans in developed nations could hope to live until they were about 50 years old. This was a great advancement from the 22-32 years that we had been estimating from birth since the dawn of time.

Prehistoric data and research suspects that Paleolithic and Neolithic people had a chance of living until they were 22-32 years old, at birth. If they lived until 15 that estimate rose to about 50. By the bronze age, birth expectancy was still around 26 years and only rose to about 36 if a person lived to 15. Ancient Greece and Rome also started at about 25-30 years from birth and grew with survival. Greece only to about 50-60. Surprisingly, Rome had many elders reach 70-80 years of age.

The average of 22-32 years from birth stuck through the middle ages, medieval times, 18th and 19th centuries. With the advancements of survival adjusting those ages accordingly. By the end of the 19th century and beginning of the 20th, medical advancements, social sanitation and a basic understanding of germ theory gave way to longer lives and survival from illnesses, injuries and conditions that could not have been imagined previously.

Today, we can only imagine the difficulties our ancestors had to cope with in order to survive. Thriving was a whole other story and must have been practically impossible, requiring tremendous strength and determination. Through great perseverance and a heap of skills that we no longer possess, our ancestors built the world that we live in today. They gave us the vaccines that keep us from illness and disease, the medical knowledge to keep mothers and babies alive until adulthood and the overall health and capabilities to live well into our 70's, regularly.

As we've seen, our ancestors had to fight, tooth and nail, just to survive the world they live in. We have been lucky enough to advance through life nearly unscathed because of their efforts. What we still don't know is how they got by day to day beyond just surviving. What did family mean and how was it more valuable than we realize today?

13

How Our Ancestors Lived Together

"Unable to record their stories, they told tales of bravery and battles, around blazing fires, and sang songs about bountiful harvests and village heroes as they went about their daily work. These stories and songs were passed down from generation to generation, preserving their history, keeping memories alive." — *Arlene Stafford-Wilson*

If we go back in time, we would first experience a world without the internet, then without television, without telephones, without personal vehicles and without the opportunity to go back.

Our ancestors lived a simpler life without the constant glare of social media judging every face, decision, or comparing each of us publicly. They didn't have the distractions of television and entertainment of fictional suffering, love or humor. They could not pick up the phone and talk to their besties or parents, siblings or anyone else. Before personal vehicles it took months to travel a few hundred miles, so going home for the holidays was less than common if not unheard of.

We take for granted all the technologies of this time and have lost the importance of what we all have to share. We are born with connection, through blood and livelihood. We have humor and

Who the Fuck Am I?

tragedy in our everyday lives. We can relate and compare ourselves without any hate. We can use our mentalities to make better lives for ourselves and our families instead of alienating or persecuting someone for being or choosing a different path or desire.

We place such a burden on ourselves to fit into this modern world. We create unreasonable classification to try to attain then hate ourselves if we cannot. The innate goodness of our hearts and souls are put to shame by the insanity of modern society.

We live in the information era when one can "Google" anything they wish to know, stalk anyone they want to know more about, and learn about any person, place, thing or idea with ease on the internet. Education has become a game played online and if the elders can't figure it out, they will be left behind.

To share our lives personably is a thing of the past. Back when our family had to be enough. There was no choice in the matter. Mom could only do what she could do and it was a tremendous and strenuous amount compared to mothers of this modern time. She would risk life and limb to bring you into this world. Then she would cook and clean, build fires for warmth and cooking, wash laundry by hand and lug it out to be hung on a line. Moms earned the respect they were shown and if you neglected her, you would surely regret it when you went to bed without supper.

Fathers too were of a different breed. They couldn't make a living in the simplest ways that we see today. Many would literally kill themselves working their lives away. They had to be sure to give their families everything they could to survive and if they didn't make it another day, their children would live, so it was all okay.

Grandparents were worshiped for their knowledge and experience. No old folk's homes would they see when their wisdom was needed to make it through each day. By the time they grew old and couldn't be of aid anymore, the family would care for them until their last day. Never could one imagine dropping their family member off for someone else to take care of or for them to slowly slip away, alone & unwanted.

Very often a village would be filled with family, close and distant. Aunts, uncles, siblings and all the children would make their days with each other never far away. If anything was needed there was always someone to ask. They wouldn't hesitate to help each other when they knew it would help their lives last. When they needed aid, their family would be right there by their side waiting and wanting to help them in any way they could. The neglect and carelessness we see today is an utter disgrace to our ancestors and their ways.

It was accepted that every person would have good and bad characteristics and that each member of the family would try their hardest to be good to one and other. They would not let their bad moods affect the way they connected or lived every day. It was understood that they depended on one and other and it would be too hard to survive without any single person and the strengths and knowledge they brought to the group.

Whether you brought strength or weakness there would be a job for you. Something that would fit your particular talents. The strong would cut and gather wood while the weaker could garden or care for animals instead. Your knowledge and wisdom were of equal value. If you knew when or how to do a certain task that was required, your value to the community was elevated. If you understood systems or situations in a particular way that made life easier for everyone your importance was known. Patience and compassion were valuable traits. You could help with the young ones or help the elders live out their days.

Love was truly unconditional then. When life was not guaranteed from day to day and something as simple as illness or injury could take your loved ones away in the blink of an eye. You had to show them how much you cared every single day and you knew that they cared as much for you in return.

Who the Fuck Am I?

When you never knew what tomorrow would hold every chore or desire must be of utmost importance and quickly unfold. There was no waiting for tomorrow. Procrastination could easily be the death of your family. People would pride themselves on what they could get done today and how each member of the family could help in their own way. This drew bonds strong and close and assured everyone their place in the survival of the family.

Today, we take everything for granted. The food on our tables was not grown or raised by our own hands We trust that it's healthy when mostly we know it's not. We don't appreciate the people in our lives, we assume they will always be there until we learn that they won't. We don't take pride in our livelihoods or careers. We wish we could be lazier or that someone else would do things for us. Why should we strain ourselves or waste our energy?

Today, we are built to be specialists but our natural skillset is often ignored. We try so hard to be what we think someone else needs, often for money, station or greed. It is unthinkable that we could just simply be ourselves, be happy or be kind.

We could utilize our strengths and skills to fill niches in society. We could all be useful and our minds would be filled with pride and passion. There would be no depression or anxiety, for we would know we are worthy of our place in this world.

Our emotions are meant to express our fulfillment or disdain for our circumstances and the situations we find ourselves in. They cannot be ignored and should be explored. We should not be so quick to judge or try to eliminate our emotions because they express our actual existence and how satisfied we are in our lives.

We may not have always been able to change our ways or the state of our lives but through connection and dedication to each other we did survive and make the best of our time. We have every option at our fingertips now but find ourselves lost amongst it all. We cannot even choose what we want to be or what we want to do. There are too many options.

Who the Fuck Am I?

We hide ourselves away and yearn to be free. Free of this insanity that our technology allows. Free to be family. Free to care and be cared for. Free to express ourselves and free to be just the way we are. Needing so much for that to be enough. Needing for society to see who we are and accept us for our personality.

I just hope it isn't too late to reconnect to our pasts and bring it all back. Perhaps our ancestors and their stories can be here to save us from ourselves and the future that is tearing us apart.

END
Part 3.

So, That's WTF I Can Do About It.

Part 4

WTF Should We Do Now?

I've finally found a way to make peace with all these feelings I've been keeping buried deep inside. I try not to throw shade or blame at those around me. No matter how bad I feel, it's really not their fault.

The pain I feel is generational and societal and no single persons to repair. We all must work together to find what means the world to us. Then use that power to keep us going and make this life worth living.

If we're really lucky, we'll find meaning in our families still. We'll have the mental awareness to share our passions with them and show them how much we care. If only for a little while, we can gather close at heart and remember where we came from and that none of us are that far apart. We can then be thankful for the life we lead, our place on the timeline and the modern conveniences that we share. Even if those advancements have cost us our connections and made it hard to care.

We are all united in history and along the genetic trails. Let's bring those ties back to our families and make societies that we love to share.

Who the Fuck Am I?

14

We Need Their Strength and Determination Today

"The most effective way to destroy people is to deny and obliterate their own understanding of their history." — *George Orwell*

Through knowledge and understanding of our own history we can attain a sense of meaning and importance in our life. We can recognize our ancestor's characteristics in ourselves and utilize those strengths, in today's societies, much as they would have in their own time.

We cannot do exactly as our ancestors have done because that has already been done. Our world has evolved and grown due to them. We can review our own existence and societal issues and use the same strengths and understanding to fight through the problems of modern time making a better future for the next generation.

Who the Fuck Am I?

We have learned to understand our world better. Our lives have become simpler. Many common chores, from our past, have been out dated and eliminated completely. That does not mean our work is done. We like to think that everything is complete and perfect until it isn't. Then we don't know what to do. Life is a challenge and we must face it, as such, with the awareness that we are humans and are fully capable of accomplishing complex challenges.

We have forgotten our strengths. The strength that kept us fighting and moving forward when we lost our mothers and our children. The strength to face illnesses and disease that may take our own lives. The strength it took to survive in a world without manufacturing and technology.

We've lost that great part of our humanity which allowed us to survive climate change and wild beasts in caves millions of years ago. If our oldest ancestors brought us through those times, to this point, we must have the ability to keep going into the future.

We could use the determination to survive, that our ancestors needed, to live in an ever-changing world and be the better for it. We can justify our situations as strengthening exercises instead of viewing every one of life's challenges as the end of the world.

Humans have become mentally weak due to the simplicity of our existence. We don't have to do the things we used to. Therefore, we don't have to utilize the full capacity of our brains. We have attempted to fill the void with artificial stimulation like video games or television. Our brains still find the meaningless business frustrating and less than satisfactory.

Going back to mental movement, our ancestors were constantly thinking, figuring things out and fighting the mental challenges of their time and the world they lived in. We owe it to ourselves and our societies to do the same. If we place half as much energy in success and finding our place in this world, that we do in hiding

Who the Fuck Am I?

from it or accusing ourselves of not being good enough, we would be masters of our time and space.

We do belong here. Our ancestors fought to bring us to this exact place and time. We can and must embrace their strength and wisdom and move through the world with pride in ourselves and our families. We can build societies that respect our need for human bonds and interaction instead of shunning people that yearn for meaningful relationships.

Throughout history, our ancestors survived because of the strength they gained from unity and family care, even societal care. People could count on each other to be there for each other in sickness and in health, when they were of benefit and when they needed help themselves. We could definitely benefit from that dedication today.

Families abandon their own everyday due to mental illness, old age, even at birth. Children are given up because the parent isn't ready to care for them. This would have been completely unheard of in history. Never would a woman have given up a child that lived. The child's well-being was of the utmost importance. Never would they have been alone to fend the world off on their own.

To this day, we know that life is hard. It is also the only thing that is real or that really matters in the big scheme of things. None of our belongings or accomplishments will matter if we don't live our lives to the fullest and enjoy it as much as we can. We cannot take them with us, when we go from this world. We can only leave behind our descendants and all of our worldly possessions will belong to them after.

Our ancestors knew that you get what you get and you didn't throw a fit. It wouldn't have done any good. Wasting energy whining or fighting about the things that could not be changed only harmed everyone.

Who the Fuck Am I?

Today, most people don't care who they hurt as long as they get what they want. Families torn to shreds out of greed. Sibling rivalries that end the bonds of blood. Cousins that never knew each other and couldn't build strength in numbers. The world is falling apart and all we can see are our screens.

The people on the other side of the screen are often not what they claim or are hiding what they fear isn't good enough. Humans are lacking physical contact and all the benefits that come with it. Children are giving up on love and families because they didn't grow up learning the strength of unity that comes from them.

Marriages were far from perfect but people didn't have to live and learn alone. The assurance that someone loved them and they had someone to love in return was a lot back then and would mean even more today. Our souls yearn for that connection and our minds are stronger than we think. We don't have to neglect our feelings or bury ourselves away in fear of being hurt.

Our ancestors didn't have many choices and they managed to get this far. We have all the choices in the world but are failing to see there worth. Our world is being overrun by a pandemic of self-hate and lack of self-worth. Our children are suicidal before they even come of age. Our elders are put away while we can still benefit from their knowledge and strength. The things they've seen and done would put us all to shame.

The modern world has brought us medicines and medical knowledge that saves life everyday but it doesn't make those lives meaningful and that is what we truly need. Mental health is coming along but still leaves much unknown. They medicate and communicate but solutions are rarely found.

Those who suffer mental illness are often too ashamed to talk about it or even ask for help and help is rarely there when it is needed. We owe it to ourselves, our children and our parents to unite against this enemy that lingers when we're alone. If we bond ourselves together than none of us will suffer it alone.

The help we need will come from that unity rather than a pill bottle. The strength we share when we build community will guide us through this harsh world. The awareness of each other and how we are getting through will be a friendly gathering not an intervention that puts us on the spot.

Most of all, we can all understand that needing one and other makes us strong. It is not something that makes us weak. Only the denial of our primal societal needs can cause weakness of the mind as well as our communities.

Modern manufacturing has offered a world of products and offers people jobs. Those products can be lifesaving and make our lives easier to bear. Unfortunately, the industry also takes away the value of every person there. They become numbers on a line which can be replaced at the drop of a dime. It's not like the importance that we had when every person had a job that effected our very existence. Each person in the family or society knew who it was that provided that service to them.

It's hard to justify the neglect of human worth that causes so much harm. It is very easy to think of the benefits to the whole from things like transportation, medical equipment or educational products. How can we place the livelihood of one above that of the rest? Can we find a way to give everyone value without giving up the best of our modern world?

I believe by studying the past and how our ancestors adjusted and modified their lives to the changes they experienced we will be better prepared for the changes that we face. We can place importance on the person over what they can provide while still benefiting from their pride to complete the work on the line. There is no reason we cannot be humane when it comes to our brothers, sisters or strangers just the same.

Who the Fuck Am I?

The most devastating and universally addictive thing we have now, that our ancestors didn't back then, is technology. The tech that brought us radios, television and eventually the internet has allowed human interaction without physical contact.

This advancement can and has been extremely valuable in sharing information like weather alerts, war news, educational information, criminal reports and so much more. At the same time, it has eliminated the need for people to unite. We are a social species and we suffer when we do not embrace our unified nature.

Humans need each other. We need meaningful relationships. We are stronger when we can count on one and other. We have lost valuable connections that have advanced our societies over time and should continue to do so. Trust and reliability are lost and we cannot find anyone to depend on. We need to bring back the unity that our ancestors once shared.

We can start by educating ourselves and saving our own sanity. Then we can go on to share that mental wealth and abundance with our friends and family and even our community. Through this connection and shared history, we can all build a better way into the future by looking to the past.

15

Unite Through Ancestry and Save Our Mental Health

"The most beautiful people we have known are those who have known defeat, known suffering, known struggle, known loss, and have found their way out of the depths. These persons have an appreciation, a sensitivity, and an understanding of life that fills them with compassion, gentleness, and a deep loving concern. Beautiful people do not just happen." — *Elisabeth Kübler-Ross*

Unity begins at home with our immediate family. When I am amazed by some fact or detail of my ancestry, I share it with my husband and my kids. They may not be overwhelmed by whatever has filled me with excitement but they listen, for the most part. They are exposed to those details of our shared history and whether they realize it, or not, someday they will value the information that has accumulated at the back of their minds.

This simple method of sharing my passion has brought us closer together. I get a few minutes a day of undivided attention.

Who the Fuck Am I?

Amusingly, they have all figured out that if they give that little bit, it doesn't cost them anything. We can bond over something that has no bearing on our day-to-day life. There is no guilt or aggression, no sadness attached to something or someone from the past.

This exposure also gives me the opportunity to teach them a little bit about myself besides the part of me that has to be strong or strict. They get to see my enthusiasm and watch me embrace that childlike passion that has pulled me out of the darkness. Over time, I've seen them begin to recognize and embrace that satisfaction in themselves as well. Without any structure or demands they can enjoy something without judgement.

Once I realized how easy it was to share this passion with them, I moved on and talked to my Mom. Through our shared ancestry and the intriguing history that I have found we have built a bit more of a relationship than I ever thought was possible.

She gets excited too. She gets curious and asks questions and makes assumptions about the history and what happened to whom and why. I never thought that she would care. I shared for my own benefit and to go over what I know and exposed her to a new subject that keeps her interest too.

We have brought each other joy and excitement through our time exploring our ancestry. This time together will never be wasted and someday it will be one of those memories that I carry alone into the future. Our desire to know and understand our ancestry has led us through some dark times and difficult battles in our lives and I will always be thankful that I was able to share this experience with her.

I've also used my new-found skills and knowledge to help my husband's side of the family learn a bit about their ancestry. Luckily the lines have not crossed as far as I can find. The desire to know where you come from and to share that with your children or parents is strong enough to unite most families.

Who the Fuck Am I?

I was able to help his Grandmother find her long lost sister whom she had not seen in over 50 years. Sadly, we were too late. I found her obituary a few months after she had passed. We did connect with her daughters though. They flew across country to meet their long-lost aunt! They were all able to get this final connection with their unknown family. Even more sadly for me, my husband's grandma passed just a few months after this meeting. I was blessed to have given her that closure and unity while she had the time. Her sister's daughters claimed that it was unbelievable how much Grandma was like their Mom. Her face and her expressions. The way she laughed and joked. The experience was like one last connection with their mother, after she was gone.

Through these connections, I've seen first-hand how important our families are and the connections we can create if we are willing to put in the time and effort. They truly are something worth striving towards.

I've experienced the light-hearted feelings that are brought on by sharing something that is valuable yet free and new yet so old too. I have been rewarded so many times over by the smiles on people's faces and the tears in their eyes when I explain how they are related or who they are connected to. It is priceless yet the most expensive information I hold.

Beyond my own family and my in-laws, I've begun to share my expertise and passion with friends and their families as well. Many of them have been lied to or abandon with no stories at all. They yearn to know their histories and where they come from as well. It brings me joy and a sense of importance to be able to help them. I encourage them on such an important journey to find out who they are.

The stories of our history are something we all share yet they are absolutely unique to us all at the same time. The ability to search and the desire to learn is all that is required for anyone to find a full-time hobby or even career in genealogy and ancestry research.

Who the Fuck Am I?

A lot can be learned from ancestry, family trees, historical societies and information that others have shared. The absolute truth comes out when your DNA verifies exactly who you really are. Genetics can tell who an absent parent is, expose unknown siblings or cousins. DNA is especially valuable in finding your nationalities and where your genes come from.

This is probably the most valuable research you can do for yourself and future generations. It is also the most connective and relatable. You are literally finding genetic matches who carry the same genetic code as you. There is nothing more real and meaningful than seeing your own characteristics shared in a complete stranger.

Your genes can also confirm generations of the past. DNA will show you where your family has come from. DNA allows you to research foreign ancestors and places of national origin that you may have never known of before. If your family, like mine, left some of the stories out or just made them up as they went along, you may very well find things that truly amaze you.

DNA is the only sure-fire way to connect yourself to your ancestors both living and deceased. As long as they passed on their genetic code to future generations and any one of those persons have tested their DNA in recent times, the system will connect you. You can dig into your matches and follow their family trees to find other living relatives as well as past family members.

It is always good to double check anyone else's research just to confirm its accuracy but DNA doesn't lie. If you share genes, your connections are confirmed. These connections allow communication, meet ups and familial bonds to be born with distant relatives that could not have known about each other in years gone by.

Our ancestors knew each other well and had bonds built of stone for their mutual survival. They handed down their lineages through stories told and passed by word of mouth. Yet they could not have known the thousands of relatives that we can find today using modern DNA.

Become a master of your own ancestry. Then you can share your knowledge with those around you too. You can pull in your immediate family with ties that bind you just as surely as twine. You can share stories of interest with them as well as with further lineages. With your DNA connections, you may share more in common with 2nd, 3rd or even 4th-8th cousins than you do with your first cousins. They may want to know the same information that you have to share while those immediately related to you are more interested in different lines of inquiry.

This time in history is the most advanced as far as ancestry and DNA connections. We have more capabilities than we have ever had and the internet has allowed connection and communication that we've never been able to enjoy before. You and I are at the cusp of knowledge and information and we owe it to ourselves and our families to take it all in. Absorb as much as possible, share it and document these connections for future generations.

We can take a lesson from our most ancient ancestors and share our ancestry and lineages by mouth, in person, through stories and tales of years gone by. We can include emotion and enthusiasm that cannot be read on a page but must be told to be felt as purely as is intended. We can create the unity that we are so desperately missing.

Sharing and Comparing our research, genetics, and histories will bring us that which we need the most, Unity. The immense pleasure we gain from community and a form of connection that has long been lost will be our most valuable reward. Our ancestors knew that we depended so completely on each other physically, mentally and most definitely emotionally too.

Who the Fuck Am I?

Over the generations, through the modernization of our world we have lost our support systems. We have abandoned the emotional responses that made humans different from most other animal species. We have traded our sanity for ease and complicity. Those are not real though. What we thought made our lives easier have actually complicated them more and removed us from the world we belong to, the families we owe our existence to and the bonds we dedicated our lives to for generations, centuries and millennia.

We were humankind and that alone bonded us to each other against the beasts of the wood. Now we are just another version of the beasts and have no real connections to keep us from losing our minds. The very minds that made us different in the first place.

Connection is the key to find our way back to them. Our way to pass their strengths and wisdom on to our children and our children's children, into the future for all to benefit from. Our ancestors held their lineage dear to their hearts and would have done anything to guarantee our survival.

Descendants were and are the only way for us to live on after we are gone. The genes our ancestors have passed on to us carry their faces, beliefs and characteristics into the next generation and until the end of the line. In a world that does not cherish children or familial bonds we must look back to their time to find the truth and value behind our line.

We have lost much of the customs and cultures our ancestors lived by but through research we can bring them back to life. We may not be able to live as they lived. We cannot go back to a world that was free of modern times but we can bring the essence of their beliefs to life in our own way in our modern lives. We can celebrate our differences and recognize how they make us all stronger. We can share with the youngest among us the strength of their differences and help them find their place in this world and this time.

Who the Fuck Am I?

Over-all we must find the unity that we have lost for our own sake as well as that of future generations. I fear that if we continue on this path of separation our children will never know the value of our time or all that have come before us. They will only view the technological world as of any importance to them and their emotional and mental health will continue to suffer for it.

The loss of unity is the beginning of the end of our sanity. Our consciousness is being strained to the maximum and we have no one to count on or fall back on when we break. This ever evolving fast-paced society, that we find ourselves in, is not conducive of our mental health or emotional stability.

If we want to survive and even thrive into the years to come, we must find unity once again. We must embrace our humanity, our weaknesses and all of our differences in order to find our strength and our survival instincts. Humans were never meant to live alone and we will suffer for it until we find a better way.

The Past is the Best Present for the Present. Understanding our past will help us correct our failing mental health! It will help us find our way back to each other, to a better world and guide us into the future. Will you join me there? Will you bring your loved ones? Will you invite your friends?

16

Bonus Material

Today you are you! That is truer than true! There is no one alive who is you-er than you! *-Dr. Seuss*

Now that you know all that I have to offer. Please do utilize as much of it as you can. Enjoy yourself, feel your worth and share who and what you are with the world. Build meaningful relationships where and when you can. Accept that there is no such thing as the perfect relationship and never was.

We must all look inside ourselves and share the best we have to offer and accept others for their best efforts as well. We must even accept their flaws and failures as well as accepting our own. Only then we will we be embracing what it means to be human.

We will be, well on our way, to building the best possible world for ourselves and future generations. We may embrace our modern world while making constant effort to utilize our instincts, evolution and all that has and continues to make us who we are to live our best lives.

Bonus Material Contents

1. Links to DNA Testing Companies and Sites
2. Links to Mental Health Data and Statistics
3. Mental Health Help Lines and Connections
4. Coping Mechanisms
5. Connect with Me

DNA Testing and Ancestry Links

Whether you are looking for living relatives, trying to prove relationships, collecting evidence, specifying regions of research or establishing your own ethnicity DNA Testing is your best and most rewarding option.

<u>5 Top Rated DNA Testing Companies for Genetic enthusiasts</u>
https://www.ancestry.com/
https://www.23andme.com/
https://homedna.com/
https://livingdna.com/
https://www.myheritage.com/
<u>Remaining companies in no specific order.</u>
https://www.familysearch.org/en/
https://www.gedmatch.com/
https://www.familytreedna.com/ Native American Ancestry
https://mytrueancestry.com/en
https://24genetics.com/
https://www.myforeverdna.com/
https://ancestrum.com/
https://www.crigenetics.com/
https://dna.labcorp.com/
https://genomelink.io/
https://dna.sequencing.com/
https://genoplot.com/
https://dnacenter.com/
https://www.choicedna.com/
https://www.23mofang.com/ Chinese Ancestry
https://www.mediclinic.co.za/en/corporate/home.html
https://us.dantelabs.com/ European Union and the US.
https://www.genebase.com/
https://www.genera.com.br/ Brazil based Family Tree DNA Partner
https://www.genotek.ru/ Russian Ancestry
https://www.igenea.com/en/home Family Tree DNA Affiliate
https://www.dna-worldwide.com/ UK's most advanced DNA Testing

Who the Fuck Am I?

https://meudna.com/ Brazilian Immigration and Health

https://nebula.org/ Whole Genome Sequencing

http://www.rootsforreal.com/ Ancient Migrations Traced with the largest proofread global geographic database of human mtDNA.

https://sanogenetics.com/ Whole Genome Sequencing for Health and Research Study Purposes

https://www.veritasgenetics.com/ USA Based Most Comprehensive Whole Genome Sequencing

https://www.veritasint.com/ Europe, Latin America, Japan and the United Arab Emirates

https://www.wegene.com/ East Asian Ancestry

https://www.yseq.net/

http://www.yoogene.com/ Chinese Ancestry

I think everyone should be able to find the perfect DNA testing or research facility from this list. It covers all areas and regions of study. Many nationalities and ethnicities have specific testing options. The companies, listed as such, can focus most of their efforts towards specific genetics and populations offering the most accurate and detailed information available today!

Who the Fuck Am I?

Mental Health Statistics 2023

According to CDC.gov Adolescent Mental Health Continues to Worsen. (Check this link for more information.)

CDC's Youth Risk Behavior Surveillance Data Summary & Trends Report: 2011-2021 highlights concerning trends about the mental health of U.S. high school students.

In 2021, more than 4 in 10 (42%) students felt persistently sad or hopeless and nearly one-third (29%) experienced poor mental health.

In 2021, more than 1 in 5 (22%) students seriously considered attempting suicide and 1 in 10 (10%) attempted suicide.

Mental Health ranking for all 50 states can be found at Mental Health America .

Please, see for yourself, the staggering number of adults with the prevalence of any mental illness, substance use disorder, serious thoughts of suicide, who are uninsured, who did not receive treatment, who reported unmet need or adults reporting 14+ mentally unhealthy days a month who could not see a doctor due to costs.

Visit Forbes for statistics at a glance that will inform you and possibly terrify you at the status of our mental health!

https://www.forbes.com/health/mind/mental-health-statistics/

For Example:

Here's a look at how individuals across the U.S. are affected by mental health conditions.

- **Anxiety:** Anxiety disorders such as generalized anxiety, obsessive-compulsive disorder and panic disorder are some of the most commonly diagnosed mental health conditions in the U.S., affecting 42.5 million adults[15].
- **Depression:** 21 million U.S. adults are living with depression, while 3.7 million people ages 12 to 17 experience major depression and 2.5 million people ages 12 to 17 experience severe depression[16].
- **PTSD:** There are 12 million U.S. adults living with post-traumatic stress disorder (PTSD)[17].
- **Bipolar disorder:** There are 3.3 million U.S. adults with

a bipolar disorder diagnosis[18].

- **Schizophrenia:** Around 1.5 million U.S. adults have a diagnosis of schizophrenia[19].

World Health Organization Has many articles, data bases and research studies regarding mental health. I urge you to go to this link and check it out. Make yourself aware of the world and how fragile our mental health and in turn the world is. The overview from their website is below.

In recent years, there has been increasing acknowledgement of the important role mental health plays in achieving global development goals, as illustrated by the inclusion of mental health in the Sustainable Development Goals. Depression is one of the leading causes of disability. Suicide is the fourth leading cause of death among 15-29-year-olds. People with severe mental health conditions die prematurely – as much as two decades early – due to preventable physical conditions.

Despite progress in some countries, people with mental health conditions often experience severe human rights violations, discrimination, and stigma.

Many mental health conditions can be effectively treated at relatively low cost, yet the gap between people needing care and those with access to care remains substantial. Effective treatment coverage remains extremely low.

Increased investment is required on all fronts: for mental health awareness to increase understanding and reduce stigma; for efforts to increase access to quality mental health care and effective treatments; and for research to identify new treatments and improve existing treatments for all mental disorders. In 2019, WHO launched the WHO Special Initiative for Mental Health (2019-2023): Universal Health Coverage for Mental Health to ensure access to quality and affordable care for mental health conditions in 12 priority countries to 100 million more people.

In 2022, WHO launched the World Mental Health Report:

Who the Fuck Am I?

Transforming Mental health for All.

Mental Health by the Numbers, brought to you by National Alliance on Mental Illness will bombard you with an astounding amount of statistics about mental illness.

For Example:

Youth and young adults experienced a unique set of challenges during the COVID-19 pandemic—isolation from peers, adapting to virtual learning, and changes to sleep habits and other routines.

We must recognize the significant impact of these experiences on young people's mental health—and the importance of providing the education, care and support they need.

- Among U.S. adolescents (aged 12-17):
    - 1 in 6 experienced a major depressive episode (MDE)
    - 3 million had serious thoughts of suicide
    - 31% increase in mental health-related emergency department visits
- Among U.S. young adults (aged 18-25):
    - 1 in 3 experienced a mental illness
    - 1 in 10 experienced a serious mental illness
    - 3.8 million had serious thoughts of suicide
- 1 in 5 young people report that the pandemic had a significant negative impact on their mental health
    - 18% of adolescents
    - 23% of young adults
    - Nearly ½ of young people with mental health concerns report a significant negative impact
- 1 in 10 people under age 18 experience a mental health condition following a COVID-19 diagnosis
- Increased use of alcohol among those who drink:
    - 15% of adolescents
    - 18% of young adults
- Increased use of drugs among those who use:
    - 15% of adolescents
    - 19% of young adults

Who the Fuck Am I?

This is just the tip of the ice berg.

You are not alone in your illness and you deserve better. The world will be better when you do what you need to, to get better too. Do your best to help those around you with their mental struggles as well. When you do, you are helping the entire world be better!
Mental health is human health, is world health, is emotional and social health. We all deserve to be well and the world deserves us to be well and do well by others!

Who the Fuck Am I?

Mental Health Help Lines and Connections

Psycom.net offers an extensive list of Help lines for anyone facing a mental health emergency or crisis. Go to the link below for information for hotlines around the world!
https://www.psycom.net/get-help-mental-health

Here is a copy of the United States based Lines from Psycom:

NEW **988** Mental Health Emergency Hotline:
In July 2022, a universal mental health crisis line launched nationwide. Calling 988 will connect you to a crisis counselor regardless of where you are in the United States.

911 Emergency

National Alliance on Mental Illness (NAMI) Help Line: 1-800-950-NAMI, or text "HELPLINE" to 62640. Both services available between 10 a.m. and 10 p.m. ET, Monday–Friday

National Domestic Violence Hotline: 1-800-799-7233

National Suicide Prevention Lifeline: 1-800-273-TALK (8255); www.suicidepreventionlifeline.org. Or, just dial 988

Suicide Prevention, Awareness, and Support: www.suicide.org

Crisis Text Line: Text REASON to 741741 (free, confidential and 24/7). In English and Spanish

Self-Harm Hotline: 1-800-DONT CUT (1-800-366-8288)

Family Violence Helpline: 1-800-996-6228

Planned Parenthood Hotline: 1-800-230-PLAN (7526)

American Association of Poison Control Centers: 1-800-222-1222

National Council on Alcoholism & Drug Dependency: 1-800-622-

Who the Fuck Am I?

2255

LGBTQ Hotline: 1-888-843-4564

The Trevor Project: 1-866-488-7386 or text "START" to 678678. Standard text messaging rates apply. Available 24/7/365. (Provides crisis intervention and suicide prevention services to lesbian, gay, bisexual, transgender, queer & questioning—LGBTQ—young people under 25.)

The SAGE LGBT Elder Hotline connects LGBT older people and caretakers with friendly responders. 1-877-360-LGBT (5428)

The Trans Lifeline is staffed by transgender people for transgender people:
1-877-565-8860 (United States)
1-877-330-6366 (Canada)

Rape Abuse and Incest National Network (RAINN) is the nation's largest organization fighting sexual violence: (800) 656-HOPE / (800) 810-7440 (TTY)

Veterans Crisis Line: https://www.veteranscrisisline.net

International Suicide Prevention Directory: findahelpline.com

The Strong Hearts Native Helpline is a confidential and anonymous culturally appropriate domestic violence and dating violence helpline for Native Americans, available every day from 7 a.m. to 10 p.m. CT. Call 1-844-762-8483.

Coping Mechanisms

Now that I know my problems aren't that bad I can begin learning to cope with them and the situations that caused them to arise. Coping begins with acceptance, you don't have to accept the causation but you do have to deal with the affects it has on you and your mental health. The first method we need to address, before the rest can be affective is denial. As in I am denying that issue the ability to burden me anymore.

Denial is based on a thorough appraisal of a person or situation and a final judgement of whether they are a proper fit for you or your life. Denial is often viewed as a negative attribute as in someone is in denial or they just can't see the truth but in this sense, it is a verb, a mental action that we must take to protect our own mental health.

There are many circumstances or situations in this life that you can deny. You can judge them for yourself and debate are they healthy or harmful to myself and my mental health? If they are harmful get rid of them to save yourself the trauma of trying to cope with anything that is unnecessary to you and your life moving forward. This includes but is not limited to, schools, jobs, stores, and even family gatherings. You can love your family from a distance and avoid the confrontation that arises and the pain and anguish that they cause. This is the opportunity to help ourselves that we have that our ancestors didn't, we can survive where they had to suffice.

A few examples of denial in practice as a coping mechanism include. Ordering your groceries online and having them delivered instead of going to the store and feeling anxious. Taking online courses to further your education rather than putting yourself out there and signing up for community college. Even canceling Sunday dinners with the family if they always end in a fight or you going home feeling less than.

In my own life, I have had to deny certain people from my day to day life because they made me feel like I wasn't good enough or that I wasn't as good as them. It is a difficult decision especially when that person is a family member or close friend that you may have had your entire life. I have had to eliminate both on several occasions but my mental health was more important to me than maintaining a bond that was unhealthy.

Now that we have limited the things we allow to break us down we can learn our coping mechanisms. There are four common categories that we tend to focus on some of which work better than others and for one or another. I have already described denial now we must deal with what is left.

Self-soothing is a term we often apply to babies when they are crying and the parent chooses to leave them in their crib to cry it out and learn to manage their own emotions. We can all have our own opinions on that form of parenting but I will remember that direly important bonding experiences that babies have with their immediate families within those first few months and years and let you figure out what I think from there.

No matter where the term comes from it is definitely an option for dealing with our emotions in adulthood. No one else can or wants to feel our emotions. They cannot shelter you from your feelings or fix them when they are broken. We can and must learn to repair our emotional responses all by ourselves.

Self-soothing is a problem focused method that selectively bases a response on a certain situation or set of circumstances. For example, when your boyfriend brakes up with you and you eat a tub of ice cream to soothe your broken heart. When a loved one passes away and you hold or sleep with an article of their clothing to feel close to them even though they are gone. My personal example of self-soothing is when I get stressed out from work or family I go for a hike and collect rocks to take my mind off of it.

Another option for coping is pampering, again we often relate these terms to infancy or childhood when a crying child gets pampered. Some view this as a bad thing causing the child to be spoiled or misbehaving but many child psychologists argue that it is a pure emotional support that every developing child both needs and deserves.

As a society, we have already accepted the term as a reward for "Adulting". Mom has been busting her ass all week long with the kids and the household and work. Now, she gets to pamper herself by getting her nails done or a new hairdo. Since we already know some of the benefits to our mental health and sustained dedication we can adapt its use to many emotionally damaging situations too.

Pampering as a coping mechanism addresses emotional trauma and gives a personal reward for survival. Intense self-care as a treatment can offer many rewards both physical and emotional. It can bring back feelings of joy and happiness as well as building self-esteem and making one feel more energetic and productive.

Depending on the situation you are recovering from and the way of pampering yourself you can induce an array of other benefits as well. If pampering becomes a physical self-care routine or experience it can increase your sense of self and awareness of yourself within society. This benefits your courage and pride encouraging you to be riskier in the right situations and even make you a more socially powerful individual.

Pampering can be as simple as watching an extra episode of your favorite tv show, enjoying an extra-long bath with a bath bomb or essential oils, spending time doing or viewing art, reading a book or as intense as splurging for an extra therapy session, traveling to a loved foreign destination. Really pampering yourself is just the choice to make your heart sing whatever that means to you.

When I am feeling, dismissed or excluded I like to jump online and dive head first into my ancestry research. I can lose hours just clicking, reading and learning about everyone that has come before me. This may seem like work to some but I truly find joy in the stories that I find and the histories that I am descendant from. It is a rewarding and nourishing experience to leave my own life for a while and explore someone or many others.

Who the Fuck Am I?

The last category that I want to talk about is pretending. Yes, the same pretending that children do and we encourage for development of the imagination. Pretending helps children create their own worldview and allows them to build hopes and dreams of their own that fit that view. This may be one of the most beneficial mechanism to cope with issues of all kinds that effect our mental health.

Pretending is an adaptive behavior that we all have formed and developed in our youth and tend to put aside as we mature. This is a big mistake. Sometimes our brains need that sense of wonder or altered reality that we can create to adapt to our circumstances and situations.

The world that we live in today was nothing but pretending for our ancestors. They never expected to actually live in a world with proper medical care and vaccines that would save their children from a long list of viruses and disease. They didn't realize that eventually almost all babies would survive to adulthood and that the world would face a population crisis. How could they have ever imagine let alone known was their pretending could become.

In modern society, we can pretend that we aren't scared or that whatever situation arises isn't that bad. We can pretend that what others say or how they look at us doesn't really matter. We can pretend that we have our dream job and are living the life that we've always wanted. We can pretend that we are loved and that we love others endearingly. Any circumstance can benefit from a little bit of imagination. Whether those illusions become more true over time or they simply allow us to get through the tough times doesn't really matter.

I know we all have heard about the pretenders. People get so worked up when someone acts in a way that they don't think they should but who are you to decide how someone else views themselves or if they are real or fake? I would argue that all humans act in ways that are both real and fake dependent on their circumstances and surroundings.

Who the Fuck Am I?

I personally like to pretend that I have much more confidence and that I know a lot. It makes me feel good to share my knowledge with others. I may not really be that confident that the knowledge I have is useful or that anyone else will benefit from it. I may not really know a lot but I do know some things that others don't and that is enough to share.

By putting myself out here, writing this book for you, I am able to build my confidence and rehash old theories. I can become aware of new details that maybe I have always known or am just now beginning to understand. I am learning from this experience as much as I am teaching it and that is what it is to be human.

With awareness that suffering is real and true for all people both past and present and a knowledge of several coping mechanisms to deal with that suffering we must now classify ourselves into the categories of life.

Who the Fuck Am I?

Connect with Me

<u>Ancestors for Sanity</u> Come over to Substack, a newsletter/email subscription service where I connect directly with my audience! I like to share my writing process as well as my day-to-day ups and downs. I express my feelings & emotions, thoughts and understandings with you all and love to welcome and end on a gratifying complimentary note! Click the link above or go to Substack.com and search for Ancestors for Sanity!

<u>Facebook</u> You can also get a bit more personal and find me on facebook. This is my personal page on which I have shared my entire life for over a decade. You can see my family, friends, vacation pics etc.!! I try not to post to much depressing stuff, but I'm sure, if you look hard enough, you'll find a few days over the years!

<u>Twitter</u> You can tweet me on twitter. Not as active as I'd like to be but I get notifications. So, if that's your platform of comfort. Please, Do Find Me There and I will be glad to tweet you back!

<u>Instagram</u> You can also find me on Instagram. Particularly, I like to post my inspirational quotes of the day but sometimes I also share photos and other pics! I'd love to have you see me over there too.

In addition, I will be adding my Amazon KDP authors page here, when I have it all set up and running!

END
Part 4.

*So, That's
WTF We Should Do
Now.*

ABOUT THE AUTHOR

I am just me. That is all I can be. I am a wife and mother. I am a daughter, granddaughter, great granddaughter, etc. etc. etc. I have found myself and my heritage through modern DNA testing and ancestry research. I have dealt with my own mental health struggles and found a place to call my own in this world.

My infatuation with my ancestry and DNA has led me to write this book in hopes that all the information I have put together can help one of you or all of you with your own family devastation, mental health and surviving this thing we call life!